Conversation Amoureuse

Jacques Lusseyran

RUDOLF STEINER COLLEGE PRESS

Original edition: © 1990 Les Trois Arches
24, avenue des Tilleuls, 78400 Chatou, France
ISBN 2-904991-42-5

Cover Art: Odilon Redon, "La Naissance de Vénus"
Musée du Petit Palais Paris
Photo credit: © Photothéque
des musées de la Ville de Paris/cliché: P. Pierrain
1998

The original French edition of this work bears the title *Conversation Amoureuse*. This edition was translated by René M. Querido and received editorial attention from Claude Julien and Judith Blatchford.

All Rights Reserved. No part of this book may be copied in any form whatsoever without the written consent of the publisher.

© 1998 Rudolf Steiner College Press
9200 Fair Oaks Blvd.
Fair Oaks, CA. 95628 U.S.A.

ISBN 0-945803-31-1

Preface to the English Edition

Biographical Notes

As you begin reading this remarkable book, it may be helpful to know that Jacques Lusseyran, born in Paris in 1924, became blind at eight years of age, the result of a piercing of one eye and the tearing of the retina of the other eye in an accident. He nevertheless developed unparalleled capacities of "inner seeing," which he described as an inner light that allowed him to see things in the outer world, though in a manner quite different from the rest of us. He was, under certain explicit circumstances, able to experience inner images revelatory of the outer world. These images did not replicate the visual picture of the things and persons in his presence but were nonetheless distinctive colors and forms. For example, he describes meeting a girl when he was around eight years old, seeing her inwardly as a "bright and red" form. For these images to be present, and to convey aspects of the outer world and not just his own subjective images, two conditions were necessary: first, he had to be free of fear, anger, jealousy, impatience, and all disruptive emotions; and second, he had to cease living as if things and people were displayed in front of him and begin to live within them—a condition of living the reality of love fully consciously. The acuity of his senses of touch, hearing, and smell also intensified, subject to the same conditions. The development of this discipline of love allowed him to come to understand that the way we typically divide the world into an inner world and an outer world is but a preconceived idea; things outside do not exist unless you go to meet them, and things inside cannot be clearly seen unless those outside are allowed to enter. There is only one world.

A second fact of some importance in approaching the present book is that in 1941, at the age of seventeen, Jacques Lusseyran organized an important student resistance group during the Nazi occupation of Paris, a group that eventually numbered over 2000. In 1943 this resistance group was betrayed by one of its members, and Lusseyran, along with many others, was captured and imprisoned at Buchenwald. The whole of this individual's life, it seems, was lived under the signature of courage. He wrote exquisitely of his love of life in a previous book, *And There Was Light.* Another significant work of his that has been translated from the French is *Against the Pollution of the I*, a paper he was on the way to present at a conference on July 27, 1971, when he and his wife were killed in an automobile accident.

Love in the Age of the Consciousness Soul

Conversation Amoureuse may well prove to be among this century's most consequential writing concerning the mysteries of love. For here, we have something entirely new, something completely unspoken of before. Certainly Jacques Lusseyran, with his highly developed sensitivities, has plunged into the depths of love as few before have done, but there is even more. He recognizes that the very possibility of love is in danger of being lost due to the kind of consciousness now experienced by most human beings. We are able to separate ourselves from the world and from others, and even from ourselves and become mere spectators to all that happens. This mode of consciousness came into ascendance in the fifteenth century, with the dawning of what Rudolf Steiner describes as the age of the consciousness soul. This "separated" mode of consciousness brings us the gifts of scientific understanding and technical control, but it also produces the risk that we human beings will also approach one another as objects and will increasingly think, feel and act out of such a degraded comprehension. There is no deliverance from this kind of consciousness, but there are healthy ways of living within it. The capacity to observe objectively finds its easiest route when it comes to penetrating the physical world. This capacity runs amok only when it stops short there, producing an exclusively materialistic outlook. We must go even deeper into this mode of consciousness and discover how to observe the invisible along with the visible, the soul and spirit along with the physical. And this way of looking needs to be done without falsely dividing body, soul, and spirit. Can this challenge be met? In the arena of love, Jacques Lusseyran has gone far indeed in meeting this charge.

Living in the consciousness soul, as humanity for the most part now does, additionally means that we are aware of not only outer things but also inner experiences as if they existed independently of any source from which they arise. There is a certain naiveté to this kind of consciousness, but one that cannot be helped. We see the trees, the mountains, the plants, the animals, and other human beings. Perceived through the senses, all this reality seems simply to exist, to be there before us and around us, but it is not possible, through ordinary sensory experience, to see that this reality is connected to a source, an origin, an ongoing creative wellspring. We can imagine that behind all this reality we perceive through the senses there does exist a source. But we cannot perceive what is bringing reality into its visibility. Our perceptions of inner states are subjected to the same estrangement. With respect to the topic of this book, love, it too simply seems to be there, and we are unable to have an experience of its origin. We develop psychological, physiological, or neurological theories to explain its beginnings, but have no actual experience, no connection with its source. Lusseyran has gone a long way, however, toward showing us how to go through the limitations of spectator consciousness and begin the great restoration of love.

Lusseyran enters his meditations on love through the door of the particular mystery of the love of a man for a woman. He speaks intensely and deeply of his own experiences of love, not of love in general. This delineation does not count as a limitation, for where else is one to begin except with who one is? Of course, it is possible to imagine someone entering the great mystery in other ways, but for Lusseyran, his manner of approaching the question of love came out of a kind of necessity; he tells us that from at least age five he felt a deep attraction, a wonderment, in the presence of girls. His attraction consisted of far more than precocious sexuality, and is better described as an intense interest in that half of the world that remains closed to each of us, the world-experience of one's countergender; if a bridge cannot be found to this other half, then one is fated to remain forever incomplete. The whole of this book can be read as a search, an adventure to discover the half of the world that remains closed to us by virtue of being either man or woman.

Love can certainly cross the boundary to the unknown half of the world; but, in this age of the consciousness soul, we are left completely to ourselves to find out what love may be. And we find that it shows many faces. We may encounter the love that is infatuation, a kind of love that is not so much an encounter with another person as it is a meeting with love itself. The early pages of this book describe the beauty and confusions of such an experience, met by Lusseyran when he was sixteen years old. For a man, this experience is a meeting of the feminine within oneself for the first time, and for a woman it is a meeting of the masculine within herself. But we need the other for this meeting with ourselves. A peculiar familiarity characterizes this meeting, and in it we learn something of the frailty, not only of love, but of our own soul. If one attempts to close the distance of the whole of one's future by testing to see whether this infatuation is returned, the future of love can be prematurely short-circuited, the adventure ended too quickly. One lives with infatuation the only way possible—unanswered, and with great and deep pain.

At age twenty-five, Jacques touches a second kind of love. This time it does have more to do with the other person. Now he meets the stranger, the woman, who lives an entirely different soul-body connection than perhaps a man is capable of truly understanding. He finds it rather impossible to determine when the woman whom he loves is present in body, when in soul, when in desire, or in reasoning. His descriptions reveal how paltry, how shadowy are our thoughts, our theories, our psychologies of the feminine, of the masculine, and of relationships. He gives a much more vivid sense of relating with an actual person, in all her complexity, and shows us that we really can know very little of another person except through constant effort. Our ideas of how she should act, or how one should act toward her—all such notions bear little resemblance and relevance to the actual acts of relating. The great lesson of this experience of love: to guard oneself against the hell of trying to change another.

Now, suppose one becomes at last so fortunate as to find someone who wants you to be exactly who you are, who wishes you to change not in the least, who loves you for who you are. Ah, that would seem to be true happiness! And it is, but happiness, as Lusseyran discovered, is not the same as love. Remaining exactly what your partner wants, even when done with the noblest of intentions, constitutes a form of egoism, of self-centeredness that also blocks the other person from changing. Life itself, to be vital and exuberant, requires, demands, that one change, and thus life dictates that we can never remain the person our partner found to be exactly what she wished for.

Is love, no matter how one approaches it, doomed to failure? None of these intense instances, so poignantly described by Lusseyran in a far more living way than my reflections could ever hope to convey, can be considered failures. I do not think that Lusseyran ever, not once in his whole life, experienced failure in love. One experiences failure only if

v

one knows what is supposed to happen. In the region of love, as it now exists, no one knows what is supposed to happen, how it is supposed to take place; no universal way exists that can be canonized as **the** right way of love. Certainly, human love does not exist as already formed, as if it were something to be found, whole and complete, just waiting for us to stumble upon it when the right person arrives.

Central to the effort of creating rather than seeking to find love fully formed is to be able to make room for the soul and the body to cohere in the same earthly dimensions. The awakening of sexuality in adolescence signals the arousal of the soul-body, an awakening that so frightens us that a kind of split immediately occurs, separating our form into two separate components—a soul component (dreams), and a body component (desires). A man *dreams*, not so much of the perfect woman, but of the luminous feminine, a dream that, for the most part exists only partly consciously. He *desires* the flesh and blood woman. And a woman, does she not experience the same division in counterfashion? Love has a hard time of it, however, as long as dream and desire live a separate existence.

The Domain of Desire

The chapters focusing specifically on the sexuality of love delve further into the question of desire and how, for the man in particular, love and desire are often confused. While Lusseyran does not go into what the situation might be for a woman, isn't it that the dream and love are often more confused for her? We certainly have to be careful not to slice up the problems of love so neatly into two piles, one belonging to men and the other to women. But, Lusseyran's experiences are those of a man; he is clear that this is his given perspective, the one he knows by virtue of his own being. His stories of experiences with fellow prisoners at Buchenwald, where he became the confidant of men who wanted to speak of their wives or their lovers, further emphasize that we are presented with a man's point of view concerning love. That point of view does not stop us from understanding some dimensions of love itself. These days, with the men's movement and the upsurge of feminism, it is altogether too easy to forget that it is really possible, and actually a necessity, for the sexes to come to deeper understandings of love by deeply listening to each other. Of course, what is spoken, on either side, must go beyond surfaces, beyond mere opinions and haggle. Lusseyran avoids these traps by keeping his focus completely on love.

We are bound to be totally refreshed by seeing someone take on the problem of desire in order to keep questions of love between a man and a woman located in the actual arena where they are lived, our bodies. So much hinges on desire that seems as though it should not; it verifies the actual physical presence of love, assures that we are not just living an abstract idea—ours, or those of the philosophers, the theologians, or the educators. How something so lofty as love chooses to announce itself as an urge, an impulse, an attraction—that forever remains a mystery. But, this enigma is the given with which we must struggle and come to terms. You may be shocked to see in print what Lusseyran says concerning sexual desire. He takes what others often present as disparaging about the way in which men live desire and verifies that it is all quite true. It becomes problematic only if lived without sensitivity and reflection. It is quite true that men have a tendency to take desire to be love; when desire goes, love seems to have disappeared. Men are given the task of working through this confusion, not avoiding it or pretending it does not exist. It is also quite true that for men, the sense of self, of identity as a man, is tied into feeling the potency of their sex organ. The tremendous challenge presented in love's announcing itself in this way in the body of man is how to cross the boundary between desire, which is not about loving another but about loving oneself, to, through desire, discovering love for another.

Lusseyran does not say that the only way for man to come to love is through desire. We must remain clear about the terrain he has chosen to consider so that we will not feel scandalized. He chooses to speak of sexual love, and he is doing so spiritually and with intense depth of soul. He is no spiritual prude, thinking that it is possible to confine love to the planes where the messiness of bodily life does not interfere. No, he chooses to seek love, in its body, soul, and spirit dimensions right in the midst of the sights and smells and touches and sounds of sensory life. He spent his whole life here, developing the capacity to experience soul and spirit through the senses. He gives us all hope in something that we all know—that spirit is not somewhere where body is not; but he is also aware that not only can spirit be found there, it can also be overwhelmed in the presence of bodily desire.

The way through this dilemma of love and desire that is lived and struggled with by so very many of us can only be found in developing acute capacities of observing our own engagement with desire, carefully noting its every turn, its every nuance, its every flicker and glow. Not an easy task, and in fact it may be far more difficult to develop this kind of observation than it is to learn the highest and most subtle kind of meditative practice. However, to develop such capacities belongs to the true spiritual work of the age of the consciousness soul. This is the time in the evolution of consciousness when we are given the strongest experience of the physical and thus the sensory realms. Our spiritual work consists of finding, through these realms, the experience of soul and of spirit.

Sexual Love

Lusseyran's concern with sexual love, I believe, needs to be understood in the context of his meditative achievement; otherwise his writing will be gravely misunderstood, taken only as interesting musings, or impressionistic images, or, when it comes to the question of desire, exclusively male fantasies. Quite to the contrary, we have instead the most disciplined description of lived sexuality along with astoundingly astute clues to finding the way to the creative source of the love that announces itself in such pressing ways in the body. To have moments in which the true spiritual love breaks through, however, takes a meditative reading of this work, going over it again and again.

Often, with this work, sentences are themselves worthy of meditation, I hardly need to point them out, though I am remembering some:

In love we are seeking, that's all we are doing.

> At the moment of orgasm a man has never been so great. Nor so alone. . . . It would be so good for you to know this. But you should also know that he does not want this solitude, that he came to you in order to get rid of it.

While we are often taken aback, astounded by such sentences, more important than our admiration for things so well said is that we experience a feeling for entering into the creating source which engenders such expressions. Only by getting a glimpse, a little flicker of this source, will the potential criticisms of what is being said be deflated. To acquire this glimpse, one must take this book in hand as a work that asks for full and active engagement.

Of all the significant insights in this work, it is in the sixth chapter that I believe we come to the most astounding achievement. Try to imagine what purity of soul would be required to be able to so closely describe the actual experience of the love act between a man and a woman in such a manner that the true wonder of it breaks forth in all its splendor. Imagine how difficult it would be to search for the splendor of love right in the midst of the sexual act and not fall either into the titillation of it or to recoil in horror that one was approaching the pornographic. The reader, following the example of the writer, must approach this reality with purity of intent.

A most astounding flowering of the careful discipline of observing the course of sexual desire the way it is actually lived comes in this work with the discovery that, in the love act, it is the moment after the act itself that bears the most significance. Through the act of making sexual love, both the man and the woman intensify the sense of who they each are as man and as woman. What looks like an act of union, up to a certain point, is actually a deepening of separation. Because of this intrinsic component, sexual love can easily turn into a kind of struggle for power, each individual attempting to verify his or her own existence; that happens when making love is not experienced in its spiritual dimensions. One side of desire seeks this enhancement of the lower ego. Another side, however, seeks to break through to the higher self, one's ultimate, true identity. This possibility occurs because even while the enhancement of self goes on, it is at the same time the self's own dissolution. It is perhaps not the ecstasy of orgasm that counts as a quasi spiritual experience, but that the moment of ecstasy announces the possibility of something more. To take sexual ecstasy in itself as something spiritual only falsely elevates the ego. The penetration of the woman by the man and the enfolding of the man in the woman already crosses the border that divides one from the other—and, in fact, for a few moments, each becomes the other. One does not just intimately experience the other, but a kind of exchange occurs, an exchange that can be experienced to the extent that love is not an assault. Lusseyran says:

> If a man were always a man from the beginning to the end of lovemaking and if he were only that, and if the woman would remain woman eternally, there would be no love. . . . Instead there would be this irritable, impoverished substitute: desire.

It is when desire is completed that the moment of union occurs, for then there is a true resting with each other without any longer a seeking, without the element of want. Desire then hovers around the couple in its true spiritual nature, blessing this unutterable moment of engagement.

Knowing Love

This book not only takes us into entirely new considerations of love but it also lights up the difficulties of living in the age of the consciousness soul and shows the possibility of living within this kind of consciousness in a healthy way. Consciousness has so evolved that it can now look at love, desire love, imagine it, think about it as if it were a reality existing completely on its own. Love, however, can only be known through loving. It is not an object existing as others exist. Living the illusion that it is an object also means that it is possible to engage in love in a completely detached manner, thus using it for purposes other than love—for mere pleasure, power, as an addiction, self-verification, abuse, pornography. Or, another kind of detachment is also possible: one that arises when others tell us of love that is beyond our grasp, love of the cosmic variety. A corollary of this distancing which makes of love something to look at is that we enter into the illusion of love, whatever it may be, is essentially the same for everybody, and if it is not, then it should be. If love is an object, something to go looking for and to find, then it must be the same kind of object for everyone.

At the same time that we might hold to a belief in love existing as an object, there is another, paradoxical side to living in the consciousness soul. In this age, we are increasingly freed from the constraints of external authority and left more and more to wrestle with our individual experience. Certainly we are now freed from the external constraint of trying to love the way someone, some institution, or society itself tells us to love. So, here is the paradox—love seems to be something objective, and simultaneously love is completely ours, to be created out of our own inner solitude; and no one can tell us what it is or means, for it will be and mean something quite different for different people.

Lusseyran's answer to this terribly difficult dilemma needs a good deal of contemplation:

> Love has not been made for the community. And to look at it doesn't mean looking at others doing it, but to look at oneself doing it.

He is saying that society, organized religion, education, family, tradition—these forms can no longer tell us how to live the reality of love. In this sense, love does not belong to the community. And, if we are in this position of consciousness that looks, then the way through it is to stop looking at others and begin looking at ourselves. Brilliant! We cannot sidestep the consciousness soul without inadvertently stepping into atavistic versions of love from the past. We have to go through this kind of consciousness. Our desire to love is now more like a kind of empty intention; we do not and cannot know what love is except by doing it. By doing what we do not know we are doing, but have the intention to do—that is the course love must now take, the course of adventure, filled with doubt, apprehension, very little happiness, a great deal of emptiness, but the joy that comes with reinvention. The condition under which this new approach to love opens up a new horizon for humanity is that both soul and body have equal value. One is never, not for an instant, lived as having more worth than the other. We must become observers of our body and of our soul life, both together. Lusseyran's observations here form the basis for a true spiritual psychology of body, soul, and spirit, one which does not divide and separate and which nevertheless clearly understands their differences and mutual relationship. Even the sexual organs are taken into this understanding, which must be the case if one is to avoid speaking of body, soul, and spirit abstractly.

Once one has stepped, in a fully conscious way, into the consciousness soul, not only love but everything surrounding love between a man and a woman has to be considered anew. Everything concerning love has to be reinvented, which does not mean made up, but rather, revisioned in light of this kind of consciousness. The question of faithfulness in love arises. As with love itself, one must tread the perilous line—faithfulness is not like a thing that can be possessed. One can no longer really say, "I will be forever faithful." At best, one can say, "I want that to happen." And marriage no longer takes care of the problem, seeming to insure that faithfulness will take place and that if it does not the marriage is broken. Indeed, in a certain way, marriage no longer exists, at least not in the way that it used to; it, too, has to be reinvented by each individual, each couple, daily. Please understand: there is not an option. The alternative is to love without living love, to enact patterns that no longer give life and, more importantly, do not bring anything creative into the world. For love to try to exist as it did in the past turns it now into a commodity, a commodity filled with emptiness that only drains the world and does not renew it.

When Claude Julien, the director of Rudolf Steiner College Press, wrote me, giving me the assignment of writing an introduction to this book, he lightly suggested that a warning ought to be written for the cover of the book. It would say: Do not read this unless you are determined to confront the true nature of your own being. He is quite right.

Robert Sardello, Ph.D.
The School of Spiritual Psychology

Preface to the French Edition

Ich bin Du
I am you

Novalis

This book, *Conversation Amoureuse*, of Jacques Lusseyran, who died accidentally July 27, 1971 at age 47, presents us with a glowing text on love.

"I've always had a passion for love," confides the author; "at age five, when I was told that I was going to see a little girl, my heart would tremble, and my body would jump."

What is more extraordinarily mysterious than love, so mysterious—and so simple— that all human beings seek with tenacity to live the experience of this paradox: how to be the other, be in the other, and at the same time to let the other be "me" and "in me?" Supported by an astonishing faculty for analysis of human relations, Lusseyran went to seek an answer in psychological experience as well as in that of the physical union of man and woman, where souls and bodies attract and repel each other in happiness and suffering.

A tragic circumstance of his destiny rendered him blind at age eight. The outer light vanished. It was immediately replaced by an inner light. He began to "see" phenomena in their most secret qualities, those that are usually flattened by the brutality of physical-sensible vision.

"I have become blind and the sun has turned back on itself. It left its physical sky, it jumped into me, it remains there, it shines there." The seer casts a distracted gaze on the illusory appearance that envelopes beings and things. He believes that "he sees," and contents himself with this assurance. If he wants to progress toward the act of true knowledge, he must tear the veil of what is solid which cloaks reality with darkness. For Lusseyran, the non-seer, the situation is reversed: he must protect himself from vertigo in front of the abyss which his eyes of light, open on the invisible, dig. To love, for the seer, is to seek the Other. For the non-seer, it is to pray that the Other succeeds in piercing his thick envelopes.

Through this book, written in a subtle style, detailed, always in search of the right expression which will transmit experiences of a rare subtlety, our eyes are clothed in the inner light of a blind man who sees the invisible—and tries hard to make us live these experiences. He looks at the world through true light; he loves love, with true color. It is about this light, this warmth, that the poet speaks to us when he describes "the gracious Sun of the Night" (Novalis, "Hymn to the Night" I) which rays out from the One who said "I am the Light of the world."

In these "*conversations amoureuses*" with his wife, he makes that light shine on the psychological or physical relations that he had with "the Woman," right from his very early childhood. This fine analysis brings forth the two primary qualities of the French soul: intellectual soul imprinted with a need for clarity, and heart soul, raying out sweet warmth. Moved by an uncompromising sincerity, he dares to look at love on all levels, right down to sexual relations in the act of physical union. In doing so, he shows himself as an eminent man of our time who wants to bring consciousness even into the further recesses of the being, into the dark kingdoms of instinct which impels man and woman to unite. Why undertake this, one could ask, and why in this way, so opposed to the usual eroticism?

> I knew that one shouldn't hide the physical act of love any longer, because that game was repugnant. I knew we had to look at it *differently*, simply to look at it. I prefer our manner today, accepting more readily our risks than the lies of the past, *but love is in danger.* I see clearly that it is in danger.*

Lusseyran looks at love—and describes it without any make-up or prudishness, because it is threatened right in its most earthly forms. Because also the man and the woman live there, together, a drama, a tragedy in a starry heaven of happiness. Everything depends on the man and the woman, therefore the clear presentation of his experience of desire, of pleasure which prepare and accompany the physical act and resound after it. Flesh can become, through love, light in warmth. To love is not enough any longer, we have to begin to "love Love."

How can one live the experience of a physical union, in a sacred act of human-divine love, which would be at the same time Knowledge? Should we practice it without consciousness or set it aside by renouncing it? Here the human being of our time finds himself at a crossroad: to renounce the flesh or to give in to it without a conscious spiritual dimension; or, to want to be a human being, conscious right down into incarnation.

In reading this book, we perceive that all the virtues cultivated in the past, sheltered from physical ties—chastity, modesty, purity, respect for the other, spiritual love—can find their places or, even better, be developed in the intimate man-woman relationship. Everything will depend on the presence of Love in its most elevated sense, before, during, and after the act. To love becomes a reality which transfigures the totality of what is real.

What does Rudolf Steiner's Spiritual Science tell us about that? In his book, *Cosmic Memory,* he approaches this question, in the chapter, "Extrusion of the Moon." After having demonstrated that the forces of reproduction surrounded human beings, at the beginning, in a fire fog, the expression of the will of superior divine beings; that, later on, as a result of evolution, they did incarnate and concentrate in a part of the metabolism (the limbs) of the human body, although remaining under the direction of superior divinities. He elaborates:

> . . . One could also say that those noble spiritual forces which previously had acted on the still higher impulses of man through the medium of the fire mist, had now descended in order to exercise their power in the area of reproduction. Indeed, noble and divine forces exercise a regulating and organizing action in this area.
>
> With this an important proposition of Spiritual Science has been expressed, namely, the higher, more noble divine forces have an affinity with the—*apparently*—lower forces of human nature. The word "apparently" must here be understood in its full significance. For it would be a complete misconception of occult truths if one were to see something base in the forces of reproduction as such. Only when man misuses these forces, when he compels them to serve his passions and instincts, is there something pernicious in them, but not when he *ennobles* them through the insight that a divine spiritual power lies in them. Then he will place these forces at the service of the development of the earth, and through his forces of reproduction he will carry out the intentions of the higher entities we have characterized. Spiritual Science teaches that this whole subject is to be ennobled, is to be placed under divine laws, but is *not to be mortified.** The latter can only be the consequence

of occult principles which have been understood in a purely external fashion and distorted into a misconceived asceticism.[1]

To know them, the disciple lives these forces completely. He seeks enjoyment.[2] But he shouldn't be locked into it and hardened in the egoism of his experiences; but should shed light through the knowledge given by love, by what he experiences, and through it to touch the divine in the other and in himself.

It is from this standpoint that the book of Lusseyran is a path. A path to the future and toward authenticity. From this fact, the passages of Chapter 7, which border on eroticism, if we take that word in its usual sense, take their true meaning and their importance. Lusseyran breaks the taboos thrown on this domain by "a superficial interpretation of occult principles reduced by mistake to an unnatural asceticism," and shows that one can take responsibility for oneself completely, right down to one's deepest forces—confronting at the same time the very real dangers born out of this process.

Don't the Rose Crosses say: to know—to want—to dare—to remain silent? Yes, one has to know how to see and want to dare, and then to remain silent. Because in this domain all chattering is destructive and negative, more than in any other realm.

Novalis knows how to want to dare. He clearly lays the basis of such a path. First the ambience of Love is created in the human soul when it makes live in itself that "there is only one temple in the world and it is the human body. Nothing is more sacred than this august form. Reverence before the human being is an homage rendered to this revelation in the flesh" (Novalis, *Fragments*). Then in the same Fragment, he adds: "One touches Heaven when one touches the human body."

The healthy psycho-spiritual basis of a physical connection being laid, love and respect for the human body, veneration before this stage of the descent of the soul into the body and the elevation of the body toward the soul:

As the woman is *the most elevated visible nourishment*, the most august, which assures *the transition from the body to the soul, likewise also the sexual organs are the most elevated outer organs* which assure the transition from visible organs to invisible organs."

The gaze—(speech)—hands that touch each other—the kiss—breasts that touch each other—the sexual parts that one touches—the act of embracing—they all are rungs of the ladder on which the soul descends; and in reverse the body rises on a different ladder up to the embrace: movement of temperature, flaring—the act.

In the act, soul and body *touch each other*—chemical or galvanic contact—or electrical—or fiery—the soul eats the body (and digests it?) instantly—the body receives the soul (and engenders it!) instantly. (Novalis)

Jacques Lusseyran places himself in the experience of this total love which can, in its warmth-light, elevate everything, thanks to its magical ideal. In the immense respect of the other, in the veneration of the body, in what lives in the body, the soul and the spirit, he shows a path that burns with a flame that consumes and purifies. For love is beyond the visible—it makes sense in the physical only if the soul and the spirit are witnesses at the same time. Therefore it is only after many chapters that take hold of this reality transcending the visible, that the author leads us to the most visible: the physical. Chapter 7, which speaks about it, could be titled: "Love and the Meeting of the Bodies."

This is how he defines at the end of his book this Mystery of Love: "If each of us is the other secretly, then the task will have to be done in secret. And there is only love to accomplish it."

A glowing text on love. A sparkling of the soul. A walk on the body. A raying out of the spirit. Love is not to be taken, it is to be given. One wants to seize love, it is somewhere else, always somewhere else, far from where one seeks it. It is a surprise which enchants because it is never where we want it to be. The Light. The Light intensifies Love. Love overflows with light. A raying out of which the source is the sun of the heart. United. Two. Two differences that are so far from each other that they should never meet—but Love is a miracle. They become transparent to each other, one and the other. The ideal is necessary to love and, however, can kill Love. Glowing text, difficult, where a being has confided himself to us without any veils.

Athys Floride
May 1990

---

*   Preface author's emphasis.

1   Rudolf Steiner, *Cosmic Memory*. Blauvelt, New York: Steinerbooks, a division of Garber Communications, Inc., 1987.

2   Rudolf Steiner, *How to Know Higher Worlds*. Hudson, New York: Anthroposophic Press, 1994.

Editors' Note

This is not a book to breeze through. The reader may find it unclear in some places and patience may be required. Often the next sentence—or paragraph, or page—will shed light which makes one go back and reread for better understanding.

The unconventional punctuation of this edition is the result of our efforts to retain, as nearly as possible, the pauses and rhythms, the poetry, and conversational tone of the original text. We hope this will help the reader enter into the author's struggles to put into words fine distinctions of feeling and observation.

Judith G. Blatchford
Claude J-J. Julien

1

For the first time? Where did I see the whole of you for the first time? I seem to remember. It was a summer's evening on a hill when I was sixteen. Pierre's hand guided me from above as usual. Pierre told me that night that the pebbles along the way were blue. There were only pebbles, and the hard and fine moorland. It was the first time that I saw the whole of you. It is true . . . it is true that you hadn't been born yet.

She must have smiled. She always smiles when I speak to her about Pierre and myself. She doesn't laugh, though. She keeps her hands clasped together. She doesn't really believe in these words that I'm telling her; I don't either. But she believes in the deed of saying it, as indeed I do.

We were practically running. We had lost our way, we had lost the path. We were not going home—we swore—as long as our legs would carry us. We would not go home until we had reached the top of those hills. The night was not clear; we didn't quite know where the summit was. What had happened was too much for our bodies; it was too little for our souls. Dreams crackled between us in the silence, because we were no longer talking. We were going to burn them all; they all had to burn.

What had happened? Almost nothing. Almost everything. That morning, Pierre had found himself alone with her for some ten minutes on the porch of her building. Alone with her—he hadn't planned that. I, myself, towards five o'clock the very same day, had had an accident, a marvel: her mother and her sister had gone shopping, her brother had not come home; I was alone with her in her home for about an hour. Yes, I think I must have said for an hour. That is what I told Pierre to begin with. Later, on the hill, I corrected what I had said: it hadn't lasted for more than twenty minutes. Perhaps a little less. I can't quite remember.

She is still holding her hands clasped together. She hears everything for the first time. I am going to speak to her, but not about my own love. My own love I make with her because she's my wife. All my gestures are free. She has freed them. We are ready to work at last. I'm going to speak to her about love, not my love, but love as such.

Remember that I was sixteen. My body was awkward. It isn't that it was heavy, I let it slip among the thorns, grazing the skin without really being aware of it. But it seemed to be too new, it was hanging at the end of my soul, it couldn't play yet. Earlier on, in the living room, on the sofa where it was placed, on the sofa where she had been, she, as if by a miracle, it hadn't moved an inch. It panicked, it didn't want to. Above all, it didn't want to. It wasn't worthy of the soul.

Now I thrust my body forward into this blue night which was opening like a door. The sharper the thorns became, the more we lost our way, and the better it was. I didn't want that body any more, except to run with. Pierre was not saying a word, but I knew, since he was taking large, distracted strides, that he was in the thick of the bushes, and that he did not want to have a body any more either.

My soul was immense. Unbridled, immense, unbearable. Words rushed through my head. A day . . . later on . . . impossible . . . truth . . . truth . . . truth. I had not touched her. At least, I had not touched her.

The night wind was getting cooler. We must have almost reached the top. My body was bawling to me: you're only a kid! My soul wasn't saying anything. It knew that I wasn't a child any more. Could a child see into his future, could he even look at it ? I could see it.

I had seen it on the corner of the sofa. Yes, not her: the future. And as soon as this happened, she became confused. She spoke with her mundane voice, her everyday voice. She had noticed nothing. Had I stretched my hand towards her, she would not have thrust it back. What for? . . . Or, perhaps she would have, but it didn't matter to me. I didn't stretch it towards her. I didn't rush forward, I had withdrawn inside myself. I told Pierre, who didn't laugh—no more than you did.

Pierre had made the same movement that morning at the side door. He had said it in the same way, and I had asked: "Do you think that it was shame?" He didn't think so. Since Pierre always recognized his faults, and saw only harm in not recognizing them, I felt relieved.

She had not sat on the sofa—Or perhaps it was unintentional, as if by accident. How could I have grasped the opportunity?

We were at the the summit. The slope had ended. I said to Pierre: "She's not the one we love. It's not at all certain that she's the one." He let go of my shoulder, a gesture he only allowed himself at certain violent moments. I must have shocked him. He was going to put his head in his hands. Well, no! He understood.

If Pierre understood, imagine! If he, with his eyes, had not seen her either, had not seen her where she was, but a little somewhere else and differently, then I was saved. He told me that he could not quite focus in on her. When I asked him for the tenth time, to describe her hair, her chin, her smile—or something even smaller, her fingers, if he couldn't describe everything else—, he was unable to do so. He couldn't do it, any more than I could without my eyes. I was saved. My way of looking was not only mine: someone else shared it with me. It was love that was hiding everything, or showing everything.

We stayed up there at least two hours. Two hours standing; we were waiting for the storm. One was rising and at that time we always needed one. I was standing also because I was talking. As for Pierre, he had to sit down when he wanted to know himself. His tall body leaning forward, his long hands, placed one upon the other, beyond his knees, he was sensing himself. As for me, I had to stand up, and move from one foot to the other, from one word to the next.

Had she spoken to me at five o'clock in the living room? That is all she had done. So everything had been easy. It was when she would stop speaking, that we were paralyzed. It would have been simple if at that moment I had thought about her. I should have said to myself: there she is, she is dressed, she has a neck, she has feet, she is dressed as Pierre has told me she was all these days, she is going to have a meal this evening, she got up this morning. It was beyond me, I couldn't think about it. I was seeing her; yes, of course, I was seeing her. She had gone inside my eyes and seemed to turn them around. I had gone backward and upward—well, actually in a direction for which there is no explanation. I was leaving. I had justified it to myself by saying that I would find her again; but not on this sofa, not the way I was, not the way she was, and certainly not today. She was not herself, not completely, not yet. Perhaps she would never be. She was me.

"What do you mean You?" Pierre didn't like that. But it wasn't quite what I meant to say. Me, in a different way. How was it that upon going up the hill earlier on, we had never looked back? In order to think about her, instead of staying in town where she was, instead of walking one hundred times around the block of houses, we had to run a long way, as far as possible. Me, in that sense.

The other evening when we were all walking together, she had taken me by the arm for quite a while, Pierre remembered. I had felt the downy hair near her elbow. I had felt her against me, and there was her scent. But even on that day, she was not next to me, she was ahead. She was there where I would be when I would have become Me. Yes, of course, her completely, no one else. Her. But not separated, not more or less near, not more or less far away, being able to say yes without thinking about it or no in the same way. She having become me, or I having become her.

Or maybe someone else. That is what I had really wanted to say to Pierre. Someone else. And, that when we meet a young woman, we do not love her in order to remain who we are.

The sense of metamorphosis, people believe that you acquire it by virtue of intelligence. Actually, that is the best way to lose it. But when I was sixteen, I had it; I only had that. This girl, she became everything. The walls took on the angle of her walk, the street, the lengthening of her legs. Her staircase was the palm of her hand. The almonds she was nibbling on were words—and they were laughing. I fell asleep in her breath. Before waking I could hear her running already.

I read her in the faint lines of the geometry textbook in space. In literature, she was called remembrance, daydream, tomorrow, impulse, and vision. Lamartine* was driving me crazy. I no longer liked ideas, because in ideas I did not meet her. There wasn't an inch of emptiness. There was no longer any me without her. Yet what I knew better than anything

---

* French romantic poet, 1790-1869.

else, something which no one could have refuted, is that she was absent. Even Pierre would not have been able to convince me otherwise. He was trying to do so nevertheless, he was so kind. But she, she herself could not have convinced me. Absent, I was holding her. Absent, I saw her at last. Absent, she had her weight and her soul together, she was real.

Of course, it is of absence that I'm going to speak to you. For you know everything about this girl. You know that she lived in my life for three years, that I learned the universe through her, and that I never knew whether she loved me or not because I never asked her, I never held her in my arms, and that Pierre, even Pierre did not do so in my place, that she left without having come to me, that perhaps she never suspected that nothing is more intimate than this passion without words, without hands. And then in that hollow space, you know also, you were about to be born.

Later, later on I was ashamed—when I was twenty-five, when I was thirty. It is difficult for a man to be celibate and to be proud of it. I have cursed my great adventure of abstinence. It was love before life, it was fear; at best, virginity. And virginity, if it goes on, is an illness. But today, I don't quite know.

Today, there is you. And you, you are her, but completely. You are everything that she was not for me and everything that she has been—even absence.

What I said to Pierre that night when we were running down the hill (the storm stayed on the other side of the river and missed us), I don't remember anything of it. But, what I saw then I can still see now. The girl that I loved, I did not want to know her. I must have repeated the opposite, but I did not want to. She was too beautiful. It was too wonderful that she was so beautiful. She had too much body—I felt it; and I did too. If we had thrown them on top of one another they would have forgotten their own nature. I would have given everything to hold her hand. A voice told me never to take her lips—not to take anything at all, because this should not be the man's task. Pierre made fun of me, but in reality, he shared my view. It is not up to us to give the sign. Too bad for that virile self-love! The sign should be given by the woman. If she fell into my arms, she would stay there; but I should not be the one who leads her there.

And why not? I was seeing flames. We were right down there along the warehouses. I saw flames around her face and others around her hips. I wanted her and I would not take her. It wasn't because of shyness. At sixteen, I wasn't shy yet. It wasn't because of my upbringing or my beliefs, either. I had learned everything in this realm on my own, and the only law that I knew about was love. I'll tell you why: it was because I didn't want to spoil anything. Where did this certainty come from? I knew that nothing in the world is greater than love, nor more fragile. I had seen friends of mine touch it—or say that they had touched it—and return from it thick as horn. Fragile, and never begun. You had to reach toward it from afar, like a great mountain peak. It was always in front of you, and never achieved. It was something that had to be redone every day. So, if the most incalculable of all joys were to happen, if one day I found myself near her and found that she too loved me, would I flee? . . . But she didn't love me and I knew it well. Had she loved me, it wouldn't have taken a moment: I would not be looking ahead of me any more. Absence, future, I would have lost everything all at once. In the evening if I prayed, it was that she might love me as much as I loved her, and that she would wait until tomorrow, and tomorrow until tomorrow. I needed time.

When one is very young, love hurts a great deal. People usually don't say this, but it hurts. It bursts out in the sexual organs and the head at the same time. It pokes, it shouts, it wants to possess the body immediately. It lights a fire whose smoke closes up your heart. It makes you stupid and violent. So let her wait for me! And don't even ask her.

I didn't have much practical sense. But in love, why would one need to have it? Practical sense, it's like a ruse (you know that, even if others are unaware of it); it makes love sterile. I would have acquired it however; perhaps I would have caught it like everyone else. But the war came; we had to leave our town; there was this line of demarcation, there were three years without any news. I had been well protected. And your place, I prepared it well in silence, and I have kept it for you.

In silence! I should rather say amid chatter. During three years I spoke to every caress of the air, to every echo. I told them her name, and it is a unique one. I would have destroyed myself if I had replaced it by another. I needed her name, her form. I placed her next to my bed. When I was walking, it was she who held me upright. I offered all my decisions to her. I made twenty per day so as to give them to her. There had been no one but her. She would be the only one forever.

I didn't have practical sense. But would I have had it if I had had the use of my eyes? In difficult moments, I tried to convince Pierre of this. He, at least, had photographs, he could correct his images. He, at least, was able to see other girls, and he could compare them. And Pierre shouted, "I can do it, but I don't!" He convinced me at last that the eyes of love are other eyes, about which people never speak except foolishly, to tell us that they are blind. That is not so.

Mine saw twice every time I looked. This picture of her that my mind wanted to fix, little by little my eyes pushed it away. They didn't want it to be so personal. It was as if a mold were being formed. And one day, in this mold, a woman would be nestling, and I would recognize her. And, it would still be her!

My head was protesting, it was accusing my eyes of cheating. But if one can close them to one side of things and then open them to the other side, the eyes are always right. They knew that she had left. What do you expect! I knew love before having made love. I knew womanhood before knowing women. It is most probably not the only road towards them, but it is mine. And, believe me I didn't choose it. Nevertheless, in following that road, I learned something: not to confuse love with the beloved.

Most probably you will tell me that is something for later on, but that at sixteen, at eighteen . . . Already at eighteen, I didn't confuse them. My head, yes; but not my eyes. They had already been in apprenticeship.

Think of this picture of her that they had given me every hour of the day for three years. Gradually they emptied it of everything that was too close, her present, her way of being, her passage. They had transformed her into something that was more than a person: a promise. They had accustomed me to incredible demands. They had trained me to see in her someone else, and finally, in that someone else not to see myself anymore.

That is easy to say? One always sees oneself. But, not at eighteen. At that age there is sometimes a grace: to prefer the universe to oneself. Oh, not all day long, but every time that one has been flung against the great walls. And, that is why when one is very young, one can accept dying—and even loving.

I had not forgotten myself, be assured of that: I was thinking about her. I was talking to her ten times every hour. I was comforting myself during the night, during the day, with the thought that I was going to see her again, that she would be exactly as I had dreamt her. I wanted her to be as specific as my memories, which were made up of the smallest details, a harvest of details. But, I was already living something else. And, when she came back (because that day too came) I recognized her. She was more worthy of love than ever because now she was real. She was more different from the others than I had imagined in my wildest dreams. But it was she and only she. It was a rest, a stop. But I who had learned to march forward, I couldn't stop.

In short, I had never slept with her, and there is little comfort in that. Why should I tell you the opposite? There is a part of me that is not comforted. However God knows! When I speak to you of absence, of emptiness, of coming and going, it is not the escape that I like. I didn't like it when I was eighteen. It was not a question of purity. Even then I only believed in the purity of deeds. It seemed to me that all abstention in the face of love was guilty, and in the best of circumstances rather poor. If I talk to you so much about all I did not do with her, it is because of the dazzling, that dazzling that happened to me on the hill during that August night, and again and again, daily over three years.

At that time I was dazzled; but today, there is a great clarity. What a delightful adventure to see beyond the girl that one loves—and it isn't quite she anymore, already her voice is hesitant and the outline of her body fades—to see beyond the desires with which we cover her, to see someone else! But who, Lord, who? I answered then: love. It was an initial response. Today I know: it wasn't love in its fullness, because I know that we can't really conceive of it, being too imperfect. But it was the movement of love through me; it was its circulation, its touch which dictated its laws to me.

Imperfect. Did I say that? Incomplete, yes. It wasn't a learned idea. Oh! it wasn't an idea at all. At sixteen I had seen it. I knew that I would never be a man as long as I had not found the woman. But not just any woman, even if I loved her madly. As long as I had not found that part in me which is woman. I told Pierre some senseless things about this. Senseless, and yet so true. I was lucky: he listened to me. And you too are listening.

That story about the two sexes being enemies, condemned, I couldn't accept it, even then. Divided, surely; but in order to reunite. The only picture of love that had meaning for me was the one evoked by poets who seek to find an image of a man and a woman united in a single being. So, loving couldn't consist of having to convince a woman. If I had to draw near to her and diminish the distance between us by all sorts of clever tricks, please her every day a little more and then finally, finally to ask her, to beg her to be mine—that meant that she wasn't mine really. It meant that she was not this other part of me, or that without which I would never be a man. It wasn't a question of being in love. It wasn't a question of deciding that it would be this one because she, who was the first one to come along, was enough. It wasn't up to me to play; it was love's turn. Let it take hold of me and compel me!

And after those three years when I finally found her and then she did not love me, do you think I wept? Not for a minute (and nevertheless I loved her), because I was overflowing with gratitude for the sign which was given to me through her. I was still going to search. I was going to put myself in the right state to be found. That other self—the feminine in me—I would meet it.

Twenty years. It took me twenty years to reach you. That is a long time. I suppose that is the price one has to pay when one is enchanted.

Remember those images that rose from your throat when you were sixteen? Because it was there that you had your soul, like me, I'm sure: in the throat. And, remember how powerful they were. Today, for a supersensible presence to become visible to me, I must concentrate my whole being. At that time, it was the opposite: I had to concentrate in order to be aware of reality. The invisible was everywhere around me. To see the girls that crossed my path by chance, I had to forget the great image, and I couldn't shake it off.

A woman, upright and supple, was leading the ball from afar, from very far, from the very depths of the future. She wasn't hiding; she simply had no face yet. She had no specific voice yet, but several. She had the voice of any girl that I would meet by chance and like for a moment. She was talking to me by reflections. But I might as well say that she erased them too, and turned me into a sleepless watchman.

In fact, I was imbued with the feminine ideal, and I sensed a call. But I don't like those words that men have found in order to avoid the pain of seeing. For me, that woman was already a being. She was somebody whose presence moved me, questioned me. She was a living person, fully formed. I could not have said who she was or when she would come. But I knew what she would demand from me. With her, I would not have the right to be happy, except in a manner of rest. She wasn't there for my pleasure.

Nor for cruelty. Don't believe that! I did not feel her to be cruel. But if she were waiting for me so far behind the others, beyond the others, it was not simply to comfort me, (as far as that was concerned, I had no doubt): it was to urge me on. I threw myself towards this constraint. She was going to urge me on to live. I was already trembling with great joy. She would finally draw out of me everything I contained. She would not be cautious. She would love everything, except my own limitations.

I only had one fear: to miss her. I said to myself, and I don't quite know why, that when she appeared, I would no longer recognize her. So, when any girl passed by, I would eat her up with my soul and my eyes, supposing it was her! . . . And, as a matter of fact, when finally you entered my life, isn't that the silly thing that I did? It took me three years (three years, once more) before I saw you.

Was it that you arrived too late? In that case, you should have had the good sense to have been born earlier, and then it would have been you who had awaited me at the top of the hill on that summer night. But then you would have had to choose between Pierre and me. That would not have been easy. We always went together, and we had heard the same call. And at that time, I had not lived yet, I had not yet made any mistakes. Do you really think that love is possible in that innocence? Everybody dreams of it, but it isn't real. At least for me, it would not have been possible.

No! Don't feel sorry about the hill, since I tell you that you were there! And that I saw you.

2

You are right. There must have been a moment when I said to myself: that is she. But when? Was it before I married her?

Memories get tangled up. I wanted too much. I believed too many things. I tried so hard, failed, and started again. She herself also took a lot of trouble. I don't know anymore. And then, finally, we parted; that puts everything in a wrong light. But, I may discover more; if I do, I will tell you. If you are patient, I will be able to tell you.

To begin with, the ideal—I mean to say the great image—I was not looking at it as I had done previously. The war had passed over me, the prison, the concentration camp. Death had thrown itself into my life. Time was pressing. I no longer believed in childhood games. A woman was not a ghost.

Yes, I believed in it still. I was ashamed to display it in public. I had lost absolute truth as others had lost faith. I left it in the hands of the Gestapo, or somewhere at the bottom of my fear, or in the fear of my comrades. I only believed in the truth that one makes up oneself as best one can, on the spot, and with efforts, but not with dreams. Love was for now, it was a commando. Too bad if it was rather a risky affair. Shouldn't one stop being alone?

You can't forever live in a prison. You can't eternally let life go on without you on the other side of the wall. People

15

are killing one another; yet they must also unite. Time is pressing. There must be destinies which embrace, a being—at least one—of whom you are never afraid, whom you will think of as you do yourself, and who will be certain that you will protect her. That you will protect her against death, if death is there. A being whose eyes do not scrutinize you, whose hands don't push you away.

I was no longer looking at the great picture. In fact I remember: I was hiding it. It was as if it had been thirteen years earlier, when I had become blind. The light, everybody was so certain then that I had lost it, that my discovery—that the light is always there—I was constrained to disguise it. How could I have kept my dreams of adolescence—that image of the exact woman, of the only woman—without blushing? I lied, I had to lie.

But, wait! I'm going too fast. A lie is not something immediate. It implies reasoning, comparison,—what do **I** know? You weave it in time. You don't start with it, you start with a bolt of lightning.

It doesn't necessarily mean a thunder bolt.* Not necessarily at all. But a being lights up before you; your eyes are filled with it, they touch it everywhere. And to see a being completely, that is already to love it.

One day she found herself alone with me in a room. I hadn't taken her there. At least I didn't think I had. And she had no particular intentions. We were not people who took things lightly, and the idea of seduction would have seemed like a profanation to us. There was simply only ourselves.

For how long? If I had asked myself then, I believe I would have said: forever. There is no time when another is

---

* Thunderbolt here carries the additional meaning of "falling in love at first sight."

there with you, when that other is no longer busy to know what you are thinking about it, what he thinks about it himself, what the world will think about it, whether you must or mustn't. Then there is only the mystery, suddenly reversed, which has become light that knows, that palpitates and knows.

A woman is there. I listen to her; she is not going away. Or, I do not listen to her, because she is doing as I do: she doesn't say anything. Later on she will find a subject, we shall find one together. We will not understand one another. Is that important? She does not go away. That terrible pain—that intermittent presence of beings—I don't have that any more. Only yesterday, they entered my life and then they left. And she, this young woman, she did nothing other than what had occurred before. Now, she doesn't go away anymore. She did not pin down any conditions in order to stay. And, suddenly—I can do nothing about it—it paralyses me like lightning: she is, of all beings, the most interesting. I can't help it: she runs across my forehead and my eyes. I see her so clearly, so very clearly!

I see that she resembled no one. That is a release. Two hours ago, everyone looked the same. Even as far as my friends were concerned, even in them, I saw common traits. It was as if, by means of a small effort, I could replace them, one for the other. I knew it wasn't right; but why did they flee before I had some time to distinguish them? As far as girls were concerned it was even worse: the voice of one spoke the words of the other; their arms, their breasts were strangely interchangeable. In the end, one would die of so much abstraction.

She doesn't resemble anyone anymore. She is a person and she is not me. She will never be me. It is frightening, it is marvelous. It is particularly marvelous. Even if she speaks to me for years and I speak to her, even if she becomes my wife and our bodies become indistinguishable, she will always be another. Why do men speak about possessing women? Possession is suicide. Not even. Possession cannot really occur. It is simply an idea, and a rather poor one. And why should one wish to possess when there is so much to discover?

To touch, to listen, to explore, to understand. And then no! Yet not really to understand. That comes much later. First to draw near. First to be astonished. Isn't it astonishing that she gives me that right? Actually she no longer justifies her presence. Her reason for being there, it's up to me to find it. I see it: it is to go towards her and for her to come towards me. It will perhaps take hours. Or perhaps the whole of life. But the only thing that really matters is that there is a place—prepared before our arrival—where we would be able to stand upright, naked, face to face.

Your question (yes, that's quite right), I was about to forget it. At what moment did I say to myself: it is she? Certainly not immediately. Not that day when she sat down in that room a few feet away from me, when I admired her as I had never admired anyone, when I awaited my first gesture and her first kiss, when I concerned myself with her so violently that it seemed as if I no longer existed. Not later either, after having made love; not even after we had got married. She was a stranger.

I had adopted her, I carried her suitcases, I was continually asking her where she wanted to go, I changed my itinerary for her, I walked in step with her, I was concerned about her mood, which was never really mine; from time to time I reminded her that I also had a goal. She was a stranger. We had poured ourselves into one another. We would continue our journey together. Doesn't it give love a better chance when it is not born of a dream?

A stranger, so much the better! I would no longer make love with myself, I would delve deeply in the dough, and I would work on this being so incredibly different—so very different and so very familiar—to polish her, to reassure her. I would give her form to her. Never would I tire.

It was so much better than the dream of old. Much harder, much shorter, but also so much more alive. A sister was certainly good enough for a wife.

Yes, I did know that she was not the one. I knew from the first hours onwards, but I rejoiced at it. All the love that I would give, I would give in spite of myself. I would finally give it to another. Everything that I didn't understand in her, every turn where we were at odds with one another, that would not guarantee happiness. Happiness, I made fun of it. Suddenly I preferred to work.

I was not unhappy at all. I was going to learn how to love and to teach her how to love. It was like a calling, and it seemed to be predestination. It was not she, but what proved to me that the total presence, the perfect union, was something that was promised to a man? A real woman was there. I only had eyes for her difference.

She was not submissive. When her heart was, her spirit wasn't. But I liked her like that, generous, yet incapable of sharing. I had no will over her, and I was pleased about that. I treated her like a friend whom one doesn't persuade. Does that encroach upon friendship? No. I treated her like a cherished sister, and your sister is so close to you that her blood is a little of your blood, but she is not your destiny. This tenderness which you give her, it is to prepare her to leave, it is for the time when she will no longer be with you. The stranger whom I made into my wife, I married her like a sister.

At least to begin with. Because later on the thought came to me, and it hurt me terribly: I thought that I would change her.

That's the hell of love. One has to guard oneself against hell. And it is all the more hellish because this belief diabolically resembles love. Most people seem to make this mistake, practically everyone. I suffered. I also caused suffering. I had excuses. But it's when we have many excuses that we usually have the least. We are always excusing ourselves. Life never does.

We were drinking our first cup of coffee. To drink it, I remember, she stood in the middle of the kitchen. She should have sat down, she really should have. She would have done so had she felt as I did, this softening of the body. Had nothing in her given way? But she was not very domestic. What she wanted now was to run around town, to run with me, to find the path of war. It was hardly later than five o'clock. We were going to do this before there were people in the streets.

But I delayed. I was not in a hurry to go out. I wanted so much to assure myself first that it was she. I repeated to myself: she gave herself to me. But is that really to give oneself? I was searching on her, on this hand that I had taken hold of—the one that was not holding the cup—for the sign of this recognition that would render me supple to the very depths of my being. Her heart leapt towards me; it spoke. But what about her body?

The baker's oven had come into the kitchen. For us there was no longer any bread; all that was left of it we had eaten the night before. How much I had wanted to take her in my arms again, to handle her like bread! I did not dare.

We made for the outer boulevards. I said to myself for a moment that she should take off her shoes and hold them in her hands as she had done two years earlier in the streets under the occupation. It was hardly possible that there could be so few people; we were surely being followed. But, the war had come to an end. When we reached the Porte de

Versailles we would be close to home. She was squeezing my arm, but she hardly knew it.

I should have stopped her in the middle of the sidewalk and told her: "Stop being frightened. Stop liking that!" During those years we had all learned to love fear. It was a time to be less proud, it was a time to abandon oneself. And why not to me? And if to me did not suffice, then to love. It had taken us, that night, by the scruff of our necks and by our knees. And, didn't love have its reasons?

I wasn't capable of imagining anything anymore. Even the furrow which I had made in her, I wasn't sure that I had done it. And was I capable of asking her? To say those things, they were only men's words, vulgar troopers' words. When they sounded in my head I crushed them.

She walked so vigorously. She walked so much better and didn't need to rest. Lying against me, earlier on, she hadn't known what to do with her legs. She had so much life which I hadn't conquered.

What surprised me most, was that after having made love, there was so little question of it. The night before, I thought of loving. This morning I was talking, I was running, I was looking for a place for my hands or one for hers, I was looking right and left; I was sweeping my dreams with my feet to the very corner of the next street. I said to myself that it's not yet seven o'clock, but at seven o'clock I will force her to go home.

Nasty? Certainly not, she wasn't. She didn't know what she was. How could she have known, because, when loving her I was really loving another. This is what I should have told her instead of taking this Paris of the first morning, in its motionless peace, for a copy of our war. But it takes years. Then, to begin with, you wish so much that love would at last have a face. You would give it one with closed eyes. You

21

want to interrupt the chase. You're so afraid of being crude, unfaithful. You say to yourself that love is born, because it was there, on you, for hours; and because if she is there, she is the one.

I did not recognize her; but I too had changed. And had I recognized her, what would that have been a sign of? Sign that nothing had happened, that I was still simmering as if at the bottom of my boiler—with all traps closed—that I had bypassed the greatest joy—and that I would never find it again: the joy of surprise. She was right not to have done anything the way I expected it. She was right to have been completely another. She had the right to impose that on me if necessary. There was in the surprise, such a leap that my soul was meeting again her living rain. How was it that five minutes earlier I could have had doubts that life—this life in fits and starts, angular, upstanding, the life that runs, that is impatient—was love?

Remember how it burns, how it whistles, to enter into the soul and into the body of another. Remember, at the beginning, I couldn't think of her without touching her, couldn't touch her without questioning her, couldn't look at her without immediately ceasing to see her, couldn't look at her without turning away my eyes. When she was lying down, it seemed that I was taking hold of her as if she were galloping or standing up. If I was only speaking to her heart, I was turning her and turning her again in my hands. When she was running across the room, I didn't know whether she desired me or was fleeing me. I wish I could have learned her rhythm like a melody, at what moment she entered into her body and what moment she came out of it. I was looking for the words—or the silences—that would make her joy rise. But words didn't reach her; there was no key signature. There was no staff. She would sit on the edge of the bed, one knee bent, and remain immobile. At that instant, where should my gestures be inscribed? On which point on her body? Should I have considered inscribing any? She could stay like this for a whole hour.

Where was her soul and where was her body? It was so much simpler with me. With men, it is always simpler. Sometimes it was when she was reasoning that her desire was strongest. It was always when she abandoned herself that she would be furthest away. She would become the stranger again. Her house had no doors that one opens and that one shuts at a set hour. I heard many noises but they were cracklings, slidings. And I had not learned yet to say yes or no at the same time, to love and not to love in the same second, to turn away what was offered to me at the moment that I longed the most for the gift, to say, "I'm here" when actually I was leaving. Perhaps that is what it is, a woman. But then what could one do with it? Make fun of it?

So many others would have made fun of it, would have done their usual, would have taken their pleasure. I was incapable of that. She was the unpredictable; so that is what I was going to love. The surprise. But to adore surprise can become a religion. It became mine.

I spoke to her, she did not answer. And yet I heard her response. It was only a question of listening to her in that other language which she had chosen without warning on the other side of me, in another room, perhaps during another year, there, where I had never come. It was a question of listening harder.

I thought I held her in front of me, because my hand was still on her knees. But yet she was no longer there. She was crouching in a corner with one of her fears or skipping along, with dreamy eyes. But her knees, I still held them tight under my fingers. Yes, her body, itself, had not moved.

Surprise. Surprise . . . How would anyone know where her soul was if it was not accompanying her body everywhere?

23

And who was her body, when in making love, yes, even then, it was not really present? Fear took hold of me, then anger. At other moments mad happiness. I became mad with surprise.

Amazing how her being was so little attuned to mine. She would slap me simply by turning the pages of a book, contradict me at the very moment that she said yes in the simplest way, disorient me when putting the dishes away, or drawing the curtains, looking at the weather, and startle me. Then, she would suddenly lean on me, in a blinding encounter, with the brevity, the intolerable softness of a perfect circle—it all became a magical experience. I felt that life was growing.

I was not suspicious. At twenty-five, how could I be suspicious of what was making me grow? Her capriciousness, her rejections, I felt them fall on me like meteors. Didn't they from a certain point of view come also from her sky? Why make a difference between these gifts and the others? She gave me all her stones in bulk. It was up to me to build. I was building.

Because she was a stranger, I wanted her to be strange. But then she should have been thoroughly so. She should have put a match to all the rest!

When she left for a few hours, I would throw myself on her when she returned. Was she still reasonable? Would she still wish me to believe it? This portion of banality that she kept out of fear did not give her balance: it made her ferocious. Or with regard to reason, would I finally be able to lean over it and to chase it from the trembling water of her eyes like a cinder?

Some days I wished that she would no longer speak French, nor any other known language, but her own and solitary one. That she would no longer express herself through sentences and words but through impulses, deaths, leaps like a star that passes. She might also, suddenly, have sat down on her heels in the middle of the room, right in the middle and far from me, and announced that I was not the one she wanted. She could have done that. Or that I was the one that she wanted but not the one that she needed. She had just met that one. Suddenly at the corner of two streets, she had found herself stuck to him, a prisoner. At last, a prisoner. It was him, because he was there quite by accident. He had come from nowhere, he had come from her country. She had not looked at him, she was too close. And if her voice, then, had vibrated in that way that I had expected for so long, I would have told her, I know that I would have said: I love you! Go away!

It's because I loved her, but she had not given me the right to love myself at the same time that I loved her. She would have—often she wept over it—but she didn't know. At the end, you can no longer love a woman if in order to love you, she constantly has to constrain herself. I can't bear partial follies anymore than I can half-truths. The whole human being is beautiful whether it is made of ambers or of moss; but when it has been gnawed at, it becomes ugly. What can I tell you? I would have shouted at her, "Go away!"

I did not do so, except on the last day. And even then, not really. In the meantime, there had been so many tiring things. There had been furniture and carpets, frying pans to shake, trips, children, waiting work, remorse, explanations, the exasperating entrance of reasoning and of the reasons and their poverty-stricken exit. There had been all those nights of insomnia where, when I had gone to find her, I no longer had the strength to say to myself, "Oh, let her be what she is!" Then I was seized by panic at the thought that she was so little me. She was trying so hard—and even the night before, she had still tried—to shorten the distance between us. She wanted to be like me. She had furious bouts of obedience. She wanted to, because she loved loving, and knew that I needed it. But when she wanted to, it was too much; her heart would take flight, disorderly, she threw herself all over me, she didn't have even a breath that was her own and she took my desires to be hers. She left me ashamed, like a piece of wet rock, like a piece of wood which discovers that it isn't made of wood. She had given me everything, at the point that I had taken everything, I had left nothing. I had caught myself.

But that is too bad! During those nights, I no longer wanted her to be different. Her eyes had to be my eyes, her mouth my mouth (and we were going to say the same words, exactly the same ones, the same ones after me), or otherwise I would have died. It had to happen one time. Even just one time, and something would be saved. Either love existed, and then one day that man and that woman would have to become twins; or otherwise love was not sufficient. But it was, it was torrential! How could I understand this resistance of a drowning person that she put up against me, that I put up against her?

I took on certain habits. On this account I took them on rather quickly. Because my love for her was so strong and so difficult, because it grew each time it was not happy, I considered this difficulty to be a proof. Easy love, it was for those who had not lived. The harmony between a man and a woman—that was never given beforehand. It only came about through battles; it was the last battle. Previously, I had been wrong; nobody was waiting for me. The wonder of love was that it was this total absence of destiny. It was up to her to refuse me if she could not do otherwise, and it was up to me to force her. We would knead one another in accordance with a form. Late in life—who knows? Perhaps at the very end, maybe—but we would have a form. And it would be the form that we would be the only ones to have given to ourselves. Finally, we would have been modeled. Would this model not be more real than the other? The other, I thought I knew it when I was sixteen. I decreed that it existed outside of me. But that was due to the fact that I had not yet worked it through with a woman.

I loved my stranger as much as I could. I loved her for being a stranger. Every time I pursued her, I called that desire. At the last moment, at the moment when she was about to escape me for good, I would make a final attempt, I would pull her by the shoulders and I called that love. She did not lay her gaze on me; but I held her gaze in my fists like a frightened bird. It would escape again; I would catch it again.

It's painful at this price; but one loves. I had entered into this marriage and I was going to stay there. I would stay there until a great evil came to prevent it.

I often wondered what this evil would be. It could be the discovery that she wasn't made for me. She was not destined to enter my life, nor I to enter hers; and yet it seemed to be the meaning of our love. It can't have been to fight all the time. We fought in order to change ourselves; we quarreled in order to make peace. So then what? The evil would be when this battle would make her desire something other than herself.

That couldn't have happened to me. I only desired love. I wanted it by any means from conquest to obedience. But she, she didn't want to obey. Perhaps there was no point in trying to teach it to her. But one day, nevertheless—it would happen—, she would throw herself at my feet and she would plead for me to tell her how I wanted her. She would force herself to become someone else, because in the end, she could not have kept this war up all her life. Then, there would be our first tenderness. I would be closer to her than ever. And that is when I would have to leave her, to leave her very quickly, as soon as I could. But why? Because that moment which I had awaited for years—that moment when she would be mine—would be at the same time the moment when she is no longer herself. I repeat it to you; it was she I loved.

I didn't know how to manage; I never knew with her. She didn't know how to let me take over nor to take over herself. But that was the way she was. I had not come to diminish her. I had not at all; we were carried away.

The very last day (you really must believe me) I knew that she had become my wife. She did so as she did everything: instantaneously, completely, without wishing to, without conditions. For me, she had become my wife at the very moment where it was no longer possible.

That day I said to myself: it is she. But it was too late.

That day I could have stayed with her forever.

She had learned to live without me. You know, she learned very quickly. But ultimately every human being can live without the other. It is unbearable and it is true.

Or perhaps is it that you and I would not be able to? Oh! please forgive me. I am a little too much in my past this evening. Another day, we shall ask the question. Today, I can't. I would only say foolish things.

3

"But this ship of which you dream every night, it can't be the same one every time; not quite the same! It can't stay there for the whole of your life. It must be sailing somewhere."

She was squeezing my hand under the table. If you only knew how tightly she held it! She did not reply. She was not ready. Already for weeks she had not been ready. And I, I had to know. This ship, it was her only dream, the only one of which she had never spoken to me. And she was not talking about it to me. She only said that, for months, she couldn't go to sleep without it because it was the only place where I was alone with her.

A ship, why not? After all, I had fortresses, lost houses, doors without keys or handles. And then, our love was so secret that we only had one recourse: to walk it around from one public place to the other. I no longer counted the restaurants, the bars, the taxis. I didn't mind this ship, but on condition that she would talk to me about it.

It was too soon. It was always too soon. Her moment had not yet arrived or otherwise she kept it to herself. And her hand, she clasped it into mine. It was round, her hand; it was a kiss. It was a hand that one doesn't push back. How could one do that? It was made of thin, little bones, of tapered flesh. It was soft to a fault.

Desperate? I didn't say that. I said: soft. So I thought that it was soft, and that it had the power to envelop my life, and no one else's. But there was the ship.

It bothered me; it didn't move. I said to myself that our images are only images and that we are all rather immobile in that world, more immobile than in our deeds. Nevertheless I wanted to be certain. But it wasn't the right day. That restaurant was crowded. In order to speak to me, she had to turn her back to her neighbor who brushed against her on the bench. Her hand had abandoned itself finally. I would ask her about it when we would be at her place. We would have a couple of hours ahead of us. I would ask her if I had the courage to do so. Why did I need courage every time that I wanted to find out something about her? To talk to her about myself, that was nothing. To say the most difficult things about myself, that was nothing. But to find out about her . . .

Finally, she told me about the ship, one day when my fingers were holding her temples, when I no longer expected her to tell me. Well, yes! It was still the same ship, exactly the same. No! There was no crew. No! There was no scheduled journey. So, there must have been a port. No, there wasn't one. She hadn't thought of a port. Where were we then? We were nowhere, we were at home. Nobody would enter. And every time she, who slept so badly, dozed off.

The question to know if it was she finally—if it was more she than my unknown person of age eighteen, my stranger of age twenty-five—you see this time it didn't need to be asked. It was not she: it was I.

There was only me. You know what is the best means of resisting this? I mean: at first, in the early time, during the first years, possibly during the whole of one's life. Do you know it? I was alone on board with her. She wasn't concerned to find out where I had come from; my memories would always be mine. She was not concerned about where I was going; we weren't going anywhere; we just loved one another. The expectations, if I couldn't do without them, she didn't mind if I made them up, on condition that I would not say too much about them, not too soon.

There was only me in her heart, in her hand. I can't quite understand why I insisted so strongly that she tell me about her dream. Now that I knew it, I would have wanted to suppress it. I have always lived in a rather fragile balance, suspended over the unknown. But it was just a bad habit. Why would the present, the present time of this young woman, be my life?

I am going too fast; as always much too fast. The ship, after all, I knew about it rather late. And when I came to know about it, I was happy, already.

To explain to you happiness? Do not expect complicated things. Under the table in that restaurant I touched her knee, and the way the skirt rose to her hip. I was happy. I had never been before. I could have shouted for joy. Her knee would never move away from me. In a moment she would have to get up (I had already settled the check); but, in rising, she would adjust the folds of her dress about her breasts one after another, about her thighs, and they would fall about her and against me to whom she had given everything. All her scents one by one, all her breaths one by one for me. An incense burner. Along the streets she would walk in step with me however I walked. If I ran, she would run. In the room she would not disturb my peace; she would wait until I might disturb it.

So happy that I could shout for joy, I am telling you. Love was so simple. I had never imagined it to be so simple. It was only a matter of being there, coming close, counting the minutes and staying put. She always stayed. The other one, my stranger, left. The other one, wasn't coming, she had never come.

But who stayed? Was it really she? It seemed to me rather that it was I. A softness rested on my skin like a suntan; covering my senses and my heart. This small being against me, was like a sun that did not scorch, but a sun nevertheless. For weeks and weeks, it had baked me through and through. Soon, every bit of brutality in me would have melted.

I became all forgiveness. She did too. For years I had demanded everything of myself, of the other; now I received a bizarre permission: she did not want me to become better. What I was, it was already fine that I was that and that I gave it to her. Who I was the day we met was not a "make do" for her: it was simply what she had hoped for. If I would begin to change and respond to new calls, fear would take hold of her. She would no longer be sure that she loved me, and that I loved her. I was happy.

Happiness is unbearable. I have told you a hundred times. But, to know that, you must have experienced it; you must at some point have had to bear it very well.

Listen, from that woman came only permitted images. How can I tell you? When she was present, loving me, I was bound hand and foot for evil. I was round without a single breach; I no longer bled; night and day I was bandaged. I no longer had any faults. Or perhaps I always had the same ones: those she did not touch, which she would not have wanted to touch. That is what happiness is.

And then, she would never get up suddenly. Never. With her, it was like a sliding from one gesture to another. She would never go out alone. I always knew where she was. I had loved being surprised and had suffered so much from it; now she was warning me of everything. To tell the truth, it became quite strange. When she left I would follow her. I did not try to do it; I was neither jealous nor anxious; but quite simply, the string that bound us would stretch. I was still with her even when I was not there. I could have counted her every movement, imitated them if need be. I had never known such tenderness. Before, I was happy only when I didn't know, when I had to work to learn. Now it was enough that she would come back and I would tell her: you have done this; you have been there. She smiled about it and curled up against me. She was so proud that I was never wrong.

And if I had been wrong, she would have been so frightened! Her lips would have trembled. Her hand would have given me that soft pressure, terribly soft—the one that you call desperate. She would have thought straight away that I had changed, taken advantage of her absence. Changed! Why would I have done that? Had she hurt me? Had she changed? Would I have preferred the return of another?

That hand, I got to know it very well, I loved it passionately. It was a seal, my signature. She wrote on my fingers: "I accept you, I accept you." She confirmed to me that I was her only goal. And it was true, that young woman had only one concern: me, me. She, she was really me. She was born with me. And what she had been previously she had forgotten. She didn't want to tell herself that anymore. She loved me from the very first second, but as I was then. Nothing had happened before. What would come later, that would be too much. It was better to wait, to wait. I was happy, breathless.

You do not know what happiness is. It's true, you don't really know. Listen a little still. It is to get up every morning and to find the objects in their places. Not only the objects, but you and her also. It is to recognize that the way that she looks at you has not been changed by sleep. Imagine that: a whole night has passed through two bodies and two souls and not a single furrow has been traced, not one erased. The nights pass, love passes; she has become your wife, she is still the same as she was before being your wife. The wave of her breasts swells as high, but not higher. You have learned to flow over them.

Not a fold moved. I was certain about her every minute. I no longer needed to look at her. Do you know that very soon I no longer looked at her? Why should I? She had placed herself in the center of my being, between my heart and my memory. Why would I have torn her away? She was not in front of me, she wasn't calling me. Between my heart and my memory. But my memory got stuck. It stopped at the time of this girl. Amazing what happens to a being who forgets.

She did not like her memories. She didn't like the places where I had not been. I wanted to travel to these places with her; she didn't want it. She didn't like the people who had known me without her. She didn't say so, but I understood. She loved to forget and wanted time to enfold us so that we would be alone in time.

"We are too happy." Did I ever have the courage to say that sentence to her? No doubt I didn't. You lose your courage when you have been happy too long, just a little too long. I saw that ship again which she had given me from her dreams. But she, she no longer saw it. I was looking for other images, mine, those which previously had given me the right to invent, to suffer. Even to suffer. Why should suffering be less beautiful than happiness? I wanted to find that surge of energy which would allow me to jump forward; I wanted to know the world. Hands placed themselves on me but they weren't even constraining. I felt my back straighten out. I was going to be good.

"Take off your hands!" I couldn't even tell her that. She wouldn't have understood. To prevent me from running! No, that was not the reason why she had placed her hands on me. She had forgotten them. She apologized. And it was I who apologized. Was I happy, yes or no?

Oh! I was. I only had to listen to her hand in mine, which no longer spoke, which for months—a day, years—was no longer stammering. That hand had no longer anything but known movements. It was precise, it was mute. It would caress me later on; It would have its modest ritual. I only had to touch her face. Didn't it resemble a fruit? It was ripening, it was smiling, soon it would only be a smile. For my part, I just had to forget that she was a woman.

But she was just that! From the shell of her forehead to the flight of her knees. How could I forget, it? Why? Nevertheless, to forget it. Because if she was a woman, then she was different from me; then she could not be at that place where I found her. She would have to be a little further away or to the side, outside of me, completely outside of me. She would have to follow another path, and I would continually lose it, and then our ways would cross, and then it would be too late (she would have passed me by and I wouldn't have seen her) and then we would cross again, and I would turn around, and joy would burst forth. I would have to find her again and again, and each time it had to be difficult, very difficult. But in that case, if she were a woman, if she were she, and not me, what would become of happiness?

A lie. In any case, a lie.

Wait! I did not say that she was lying. Not she. She was one of those beings who once she promised would never renege. She had every right to be immobile. She had every right to have chosen herself once and for all, and to have lost herself in another. To reinvent life every time you wake up, why would she have done that? It is not up to a woman to invent, that is God's privilege. No, I do not think that she lied, ever. She was made for happiness.

It is I. I lied. From the first day onwards, and for years. And for what purpose? In order to console myself. It is not a crime, it is a misery. I lied in order to be happy too. Why would peace not be possible? Peace, confidence, words that one need not say, words that repeat themselves, tomorrow which will be like yesterday, everything that one has heard already and that one wants to hear again, the road is always open, it is always the same road. Happiness, in short!

Not a single gesture. I didn't want to make a single one anymore. My bones were broken by all those outings that a woman had forced upon me. My heart was broken. What I needed was a familiar being, so familiar this time that I could know it without even thinking about it. I needed clear thoughts, reliable feelings. I needed her. Thus I lied.

It's odious isn't it? The words are odious. But life is so much more innocent. The lie, it's today that I see it—fifteen years later. At the moment when that girl came into my life I loved her. She poured on me all the happiness in the world. I loved her exactly as I told her. I no longer distinguished the part that adventure played. I didn't want it. I never said to her, "In order to love you I renounce movement." I didn't know that I was renouncing it. I lied, but from such great and confusing distances that I was not aware of it. It wasn't love that took hold of us, it was happiness. How would we have known? Who ever teaches us that happiness is not love? Who? I ask you. Is there a single couple who has not made that mistake, if only for a month or a year?

And then, she was not lucky. There are men to whom happiness is allowed. There are men who would die if they lost it. She needed one of those; she found me. Because if I am not fooling myself, I'm not an example. I had already made such long journeys.

One doesn't meet love with impunity before loving. Love becomes a law which impels one like the magnetic pole that determines the magnet. I fought hard, I wanted to stop the needle. I had thought that I could only obey happiness. I was not destined for it.

How would she have understood? I had disarmed her. Or perhaps she had disarmed me first. She had given me a taste for something else, her taste. But later on. Later on, and for years, I was in the wrong. I did not speak to her of the grand image. I think that she has never known about it.

It resembled her so little. To quicken it in front of her eyes, that would have seemed to me a cruel deed, as if I couldn't have held back, and as if I would give her my shame because I was not capable of carrying it alone—my shame of having lost the image. And anyway in the name of what should an image be a law? To learn that it is one, an invincible one, you must first have renounced it. It is even necessary one day to make fun of it as if it were a poor dream. You need to have been wrong and you need to have cheated others. I was wrong, but I did it truly. I have completely lived my lie.

But yes, I gave in to the temptation, the worst one that can exist between a man and a woman: to want to give happiness. To want to give as much as one receives—and even a little more, always a little more. I must say that she had such a touching way of being happy and not saying it, simply being happy and not giving any reason for it. Being happy as if for the first time, as if, between her childhood and my coming into her life, everything had been erased for her. Her happiness, I wanted it so much. I believed that by giving her happiness every morning after awakening, that I had realized love. Love. Love at last, and no longer its images. I believed it.

She didn't live enough. She suffered—I knew it only too well—from this economy that she made of joy. But that didn't count: I would spend it for her. I would stop her briefly,

I would hold her for an instant against me, and I would not ask her whether she was happy because I knew that she was: and why should she have told me, since she knew I was being happy for two? In the long run, I had only one need, one only: to have her needs. Hers, and so precisely that she could at last forget what prevented her from living.

Because she didn't live very much, you see. Not yet, and she was aware of it. She first needed a certainty; and that certainty, the first one really, was me. So, since I had taken her life into my arms, I was going to carry it. I could not do anything else. And since she only knew one path, that was the one I was going to follow.

She didn't want me to change. Oh yes, she wanted me to become a little more responsible, a little less lost than on the first day, but on condition that I would remain the same man, in the same house, and that she would have all the keys. My departures (I left from time to time in spite of myself) would leave her trembling. She had given herself; she was quite prepared for me to draw her along. But if I were to go alone somewhere, if I were to walk at a different pace than hers, that would drive her mad. I wasn't unhappy with this happiness, not to begin with. No longer to desire your wishes, but to only want what the beloved being wishes is an ecstasy, and I don't know why no one ever talks about it, because it is greater than that which comes to us through the most foolish egoism. In fact, it is another egoism. Ah no! It is not a gift to be given. And nevertheless it is the one that I gave.

I did so for fifteen years. Then I stopped suddenly. I suppose it was fatal. But she was no longer there. There was just me in the end.

Of course, what I say contradicts the facts. She was there; she was there more than ever. She was perfectly immobile. It was certainly not she who left. She had all her positive qualities from the first day: the same obscure faith, the same stubbornness in peace, the same abandonment without folly, in her breast the same hidden dreams, the same way of being absent although enveloping me totally. She always hoped that I would be taller by a head, and that she would meet me; and that again I would overtake her, and that she would again reach my level. She believed in us as a couple; she believed that she had sacrificed everything to it completely. She who spoke so little, spoke of this. She believed she had lost herself in me, body and soul, without constraint. All of her silence, she believed that she had given it to me so that I could make my noise. She believed she knew me at every hour of the day. She had no control over my thoughts; but over my dreams!. . . She was sure that she had dreamt them all with me. She didn't know that I kept quiet. I remained silent for fifteen years.

Are you hearing what I'm saying? What I did, you should not do. You must never live in place of another. You mustn't even try. Even in order to draw someone from unhappiness, even in order to comfort someone, you must never forget yourself. It is not self-love that insists on it: it is love itself. We have our own dreams, our own rhythm. We even have our own delirious moments. We have to keep them. And the other has hers—why not—but hers. One should not adapt oneself. And never, one must never make one's life like the other wants it.

It is contrary to generosity, to kindness. But what have these desires to do with love? It is contrary to forgetting oneself. But to love is to remember all the time, not to forget oneself. Or otherwise it is a rotten gift.

These are not ideas. I wish they were. But I have lived through this rotting and I have made a woman live through it, a woman who didn't deserve it, a woman who remained what she was. I was the bad donor.

39

4

I've always had a passion for love. I think I've always had it. Yes, ever since childhood. It is very simple: at age five, when I was told that I was going to see a little girl, my heart would tremble, my whole body would jump. Later, at the elementary school, I was burning to question my friends who had the good luck of having a sister. I prepared my questions for recess. "Your sis, does she tell you what it's like for her?" How what is like? The friend never understood. He thought that I didn't know how a girl was made. I reassured him. But then he didn't understand at all; and so I kept all my other questions to myself—all those that I had wanted to ask for the last two days. I didn't have the courage. Even today in talking to you, it's still courage that I have to find. All right, here are a few:

Your sister, you told me she was two years older than you? She is ten. In the morning, when she wakes up, does she tell you her dreams or doesn't she dare to do so?

Silly question, this matter of daring. Nevertheless, everything starts there. And if he wouldn't answer, didn't know or didn't want to, then we couldn't really go on. What followed was:

Your sister, does she see the same colors that you do? Because she is a girl, are they the same for her? When she kisses her own arm, does it have the same taste? When you leave the house together, does she walk the same way that you do or differently? In your opinion, how is it to be a girl? I mean the feeling in the legs or in the hair. Has she ever told you? If girls dressed exactly the same way that we do, would we be able to recognize them?

I think that if I'd had a sister I would have kept quiet as I did with my friends. Or it would have been far more serious: I would have asked my questions the wrong way round, I would have asked them differently. And I wouldn't have been any the wiser. I had a passion for love, and there are so few boys who have that.

A precocious sexuality. Watch out: surely it was that, and it wasn't that at all. At eight years of age, I was not tormented by curiosity—not yet—because I still had all the "permissions" of childhood, and it happened that I was able to satisfy my curiosity. But when I met a girl, it seemed that I was suddenly placed face to face with half of the world. The southern hemisphere, if you want; and I would not be allowed to travel there. There was a magic line. In my family, in my games, at school, we spoke of everything, but never of this line. For the others, it seemed as if it didn't exist. But yet for me, if I didn't cross it, it seemed as if someone was forbidding me . . . I was unable to say exactly what it was. It seemed as if I had not been given the right to be complete.

I was quite willing to be a boy. That didn't bother me at all. But I had the impression, from time to time, of not being one completely, since I couldn't be a girl at the same time. It was fine to see the difference. But to live it, why was that not possible? The girls understood better, a little better. Most of them said that they wanted to be boys. But that confused me totally, because, when they said that, they immediately disgusted me.

It was not a question of being another. Becoming the opposite, that has never been a solution. It was a question of being both. Not even that. What would have been necessary, would be to have lived life twice over, in both directions, to know it to the right and to the left, in a short skirt and in short pants, sucking one's arm and using one's fist, dreaming the right way and then upside down, looking at everything the way girls do with clever glances, and lying down full length on the ground, like boys with stupid looks. Even at home, I always thought there were two households: Mom's and Dad's. I couldn't even imagine sometimes, how men and women could get married, how they went about living together. There were always two houses, two parts. The fruit was cut in two. The fruit no longer had enough taste. I wanted to hold the whole of it, to touch it all over, to turn it, turn it, and prevent it from being divided. I had wanted no one ever ever to prevent me from touching the fruit.

No one prevented me really. But I was a child, and it is more or less forbidden to all children. We make them believe that the difference is not such a serious matter, that they would be wrong to make anything much of it; or that the difference is enormous, shameful, that they will have plenty of time later on to discover it. In short, we don't want them to think about love, even if their life depends upon it. My life depended on it.

It all came to a head the day that I lost my eyes. Here! I'm going to tell you something I've not yet said to anyone. To no one really, I believe. Something that I don't like, which hurts, but which I know too well now to hide it from you. When, at eight I suddenly became blind, it was touch and go, whether I would begin to love. And it would have been decided for life.

I'm not speaking about the world. With it, a miracle took place. I found again complete within me the exterior light which had been taken away. Objects, the most distant and the closest, reached me again, they changed their location, they rubbed against my soul. I haven't lost a single one of them. I'm not speaking about the world. Not today. The world never refuses. It's a marvel, that I have said before, and

I will say it again. But, apart from the world, there are human beings and they do refuse.

I have become blind, and the sun has turned back on itself. It left its physical sky, it jumped into me, it remains there, it shines there. The plants follow it, so do the stones and the furniture, all the forms and their joys—right down to the gas outlet on the sidewalk. Everything is near. Everything is so much closer than it is with eyes. Becoming blind is like changing one's center. It is being thrown so completely into oneself that this "inside" is no longer one's own, and it grows, invades the space, brings it close to you, and then releases it and makes it vibrate. And it is the pulse of a new life. But where were the human beings? Where were they?

For years their faces have been lost to me. Did they ever have a face? What did Mom's eyes really look like when I saw them looking at me? My memory, which was infallible as far as insects and showcases were concerned, allowed me to find again the exact place of the smallest bottle of milk in the dairy shop, which revealed intact the grain in every blossom, in every stone, in every piece of bread, in every piece of cloth, why wasn't it able to place a nose in the middle of a face? As for the skin, the color of the skin, it had disappeared. It was useless for me to imagine it, for then I would see it as red, or yellow, or gray, and I didn't want it anymore. It was no longer there. It had detached itself from all the faces and all the limbs. It was even more difficult because it applied to smiles and grimaces, in fact all the gestures that I had seen people make, in the past. They no longer made them.

Humanity no longer had a form. Can you imagine that? Or rather yes; it did. But it was the form of its clothes. I still saw its hats and shoes and umbrellas and colors. It seemed as if humanity was held together by buttons. I could no longer imagine it undressing. That I couldn't do anymore.

I wasn't suffering. Until my adolescence, I don't believe that I ever really suffered. I was too much filled with the sky; there was no room for suffering. Nevertheless, that could not last. The only thing that remained in human beings was warmth. I felt them press themselves on me, very much like a compress. Some were icy cold, others were burning hot. They either wanted for me something good or bad. Or, most often, they didn't want anything, and it felt cold. It was a kind of cold that prevented one from loving.

Even in the rush, after school or in the subway, people ran away. Their bodies would press against me, but they no longer had heads. It was always the head that went first. People put between themselves and me a very short distance, and yet it was immense, like a window glass. A window glass, isn't very much; but try to break it! People had bodies without heads which moved without going anywhere, and there was always a risk that they might hurt me. And in addition, all these bodies spoke. I who had thought that words came out of the mouth, I discovered that they came out of the stomach, out of the shoulders, out of an area between the stomach and the shoulders, and that they are not really words, but a movement; one more. From near, or far, people didn't want me to get close anymore. Previously my eyes had made me believe that it was allowed to be with them, because my eyes had crossed the distance and people didn't even notice it. Now I only had a sensitive ear to give—an open throat, nostrils open—and I hoped for an echo that would be the reverberation on my body of another body. The echo occurred, but it missed me.

To the point where a doubt came to me: perhaps I was the only one in the world to have a body. Or, rather that the one I had was perhaps different from all the others. I would have to have proof. I would have had to hold out my hand and place it on someone. But not just once by coincidence; once per minute. Not out of despair, because I couldn't stand it any longer—because that would be too late: but just quite simply without thinking about it, in a moment when I was not afraid, when the other person would not have even expected it, when I would not have asked permission. I needed to touch people, but they didn't want it.

Did I really try? Not quite. In advance, their refusal screamed in my ears. They were suspicious, they preferred the windowpane. Very often, even when they spoke to me close up, I noticed that there remained between their mouth and my face, cautiously, the width of a hand. What is it about the body that you are allowed to see but not to touch it? I who loved the body so much! I who could have spent hours on nothing but that! Love, that's all very well; but if it folds itself up into the bottom of one's soul, if it contents itself with projects, it becomes a trembling thing, which doesn't know anymore what it wants, it becomes something that isolates. I didn't want to be alone in loving.

The girls were there. In a sense, they were more present than the boys. In fact, and that's the funny part of it, boys at least would run over you, they would bump into you. With them it was constant body to body, without heads. However, girls would not disappear so quickly; it seemed as if they were waiting. Only, was it me that they were waiting for? I remember this question. I asked it the way one holds one's breath.

The girls had a body. At least they knew it. They knew it better than the boys, although it was the boys who used theirs more actively. But girls took care of it. I had a hope. But alas (I noticed it early on) they took care above all to maintain its distance.

They all had the same way of sitting next to you, very close, as if it were their greatest pleasure. I said to myself; "Perhaps she wouldn't mind." Then, quite suddenly they started to calculate, to remain sitting there, although in reality they had disappeared. That one, too, she didn't want me to touch her. That I wanted to, well, that was alright; but not that I would do it. And if later on she would tell me to do it, if finally she decided, it was I who wouldn't want to do it anymore. I knew that I wouldn't do it anymore.

Before my accident, it was something else. Even if my fingers would touch a girl, she didn't notice, she thought it was my eyes. Eyes don't bother anyone. Now, if I touched the knee (without willing it, my mind somewhere else), she would move back a little. Just a little; but it was already too late; she had moved back. It was as if she was afraid that I would take the crease out of her.

Not all of them were like that, that's true. There were also those who were happy (so happy!) that I was blind, because they were certain for once not to be seen, and they would take my hand and pass it hastily over their necks or their buttocks. Two or three of them did that, the first year. But that was worse. I don't know why, but it was worse. They did it for themselves, they did not do it for me. They acted as if they were doing everything, but they weren't doing anything. When my hand had come to rest where they wanted it to, they pushed it away, and that was the end of it. It was much more definite than with those who allowed nothing. I was hurting all over. The truth is that you are not allowed to touch people, that they would never want that. And if you do it anyway, you're just a little rascal. In any case, if you touch, you see nothing, or hardly anything, because the other human being won't allow himself to be touched completely, never for good reasons, never for your reasons. From one moment to another he will laugh, laugh at who knows what—at himself, at you—although it is not at all funny and certainly not ridiculous, but passionate, timid, interminable and almost sad because it is so joyful, and you have only one longing: to say thank you.

And the boys, what did they do with their hands? Why did they not treat them like eyes? When they had peeked between the curtains as a neighboring woman was getting ready for bed, they would come and tell me how good it was. But I, if I told them that I would have to touch, they declared to me that it was dirty. At the tips of my fingers, however, ten tender eyes were born that wanted to see, to walk around without being seen, to run over everything without hurting anyone, to close if necessary, exactly like ordinary eyes. They could have closed; it would only take a simple movement: to no longer move the hands. But I had to lock myself in, and only satisfy my fingers in hiding. I had to slide the bed in front of the door in order to delay the entrance of my parents in case of emergency. I had to lock myself up in the closet, or draw the curtains and not turn on the light. I had to play doctor—that game—the girls all liked that. I had to think of everything except what I was doing, to appear not to think of it at all. I had to chuckle like an idiot and pretend to be embarrassed as if we were in the bathroom and the door had opened suddenly. When I touched, nothing was quite the same as before, my heart had taken a turn. My fingers had begun to blush. That was inevitable.

What about other hands, I would have to invent them; living at this distance I wasn't able to. To find hands which would be invisible to girls. I tried words. They were not forbidden. But then nobody seemed to realize it; that gave me a privilege. I started talking like a madman. I placed words on their foreheads, on their cheeks. I made them move from their feet to their shoulders. I was weaving dresses and skirts with them. I made up stories that dressed up and others that undressed. I was telling stories in the daytime, when one can only guess at people, and at night when one knows them better. I called that love, but I didn't use the word: I was too frightened of it.

Finally, I opened my eyes again. I did so at a place that I alone knew. Secret and incredibly clear. It was no longer in the middle of the face, in those two mirroring holes. It was no longer at the tip of my fingers that I had tried to forget.

But in the circulation, like clear water across my throat, my forehead and my head—the whole of my head. It was in a great passage of life; and this life, was no doubt my own, but I felt it outside of myself—in the whole of space one might say. I called to it softly. If I became irritable it would no longer descend. But when I received it properly, it became the light, it allowed me to look. Look! Look! They would all have a body again. Above all they almost had a face. And what they had as a face was less ugly. It was no longer as if I wanted absolutely to guess the crease between the two eye brows which started at the shoulder, which started from the arm and the way it was raised. And the line in the forehead was not more beautiful than the one in the arm. But now, I had no longer anything to guess: I saw.

I saw something, and the girls were less afraid. They didn't understand; yet they listened. I wanted to tell them this "something." But there, again, everything stopped. How could I make them understand that for me, they had eyes, a nose, a mouth, and that they didn't have them? That in their place there was a light, sometimes a little darker here and there; and that this light, if they were kind would tremble a little but would rest my eyes? If they were more attentive the lips in turn would appear; the chin, instead of fleeing, would fall forward. And the hair, could I also say something about the hair? Yes, I could: it was like smoke. A blond smoke, a brown smoke, and it was running towards me across the room. I could have blown round puffs with it. And what could I say about the color of what they were wearing? That was impossible; and it was of no interest. They were disappointed. No interest. That was not them. How could I possibly explain it to them?

There was only one means: to dream. But I didn't want to use it, because it would be false. Was I dreaming? I wished I could have convinced them to see as I was seeing. I wished I could have given them my eyes—I had too many for me alone. But then nobody would have understood. Well, that's too bad! To dream. And above all to make others dream, to lead them willingly or reluctantly, after an hour of my legends, to close their eyes finally, their two immobile eyes which only opened one horizon. But, once my legend had come to an end, would I still have been able to see something?

Imagine me trying to sell my dreams. I was only ten, you know. A girl was there. She sat down on the floor to listen to me. If she was bored, I felt her warmth, whiffs of her scent, but I didn't see her. If she really listened to me, her body would emerge bit by bit. First, the eyes. Almost always the eyes first. There were two little black wings, or blue, or dark gray, that were beating below the forehead. I could see them, even if she kept her eyes lowered. Then the forehead also emerged from the fog. It was pink, a very pale pink; it seemed to be lit up from the inside. The hair was not yet there. It only appeared at the end, and rarely, because, to be thick and to flood me, she had to be passionately fond of my dreams. Or, if this marvel occurred, I would already see her whole body, even the two feet, even the knees, even the concave line of the back (the back is so telling about a girl). Even the dress and its folds, even the color of the dress, which I did not know, which was becoming like that of the cheeks or the eyes, depending on whether I was thinking about them more or less. And I had no energy left to perceive the hair. It would be left for another time, it would be when she asked me for another dream. Would she ask me?

Most of them didn't listen for very long. And I was aware of it right away. As soon as they thought of something else, they no longer had mouths, they no longer had knees. Finally, the eyes would disappear. And then, there were all those who, instead of seeing the dream that I was showing them, used it to make up another—one that would become their own. Those never had a whole body, but only outlines of a body. It was a ball that was rolling between my fingers; or a vase with two handles; or interwoven branches and so light that the wind was constantly displacing them; or a night sky punctured by vague lights; or an arm which suddenly expands interminably which the body doesn't follow. There was nothing left but to dream more strongly, to impose my dreams, and I didn't like that. I seemed to be all alone in the world, to be the only one made of matter, and the cold took hold of me.

I knew the way to see all the girls. It was necessary for me to live in a double way. If I concentrated my desire to see them right down to the feeling of the blood in my eyes, I knew that I would see them all. In a certain way, I would see them. But what would I do with all those images? They would come from me, not from them. They would have to give me these images too. Seers speak so poorly about imagination. You would think that they don't know about it. They pretend to be sure that it replaces everything, and notably the eyes. They ignore the fact that it can actually create thousands of figures, combine them for days, and they leave you in an emptiness as great as that of a migraine. The night of blindness, I've always said that it doesn't exist. But it does exist: it is the invasion of images.

Because not all of them are good. There are those images that tell you the opposite of reality, that don't tell you anything more than your own reality. And if you have the misfortune to look at them too much, that would be the end of love. Right away, in a few hours. No longer a question of talking to someone, nor to even want anyone to talk to you. No longer a question of reminding yourself that others exist. One is a prisoner in a world that turns. The only voice is the one inside your head. You don't love anything anymore except to listen to yourself. I didn't want that world. I didn't want to imagine: I wanted to see.

And I saw. But the condition—because there was one—I understood it poorly at age ten. I had to want to see, and those I was looking at had to want to be seen. The condition was love. It is still the same today. And for all of you, it's the same. But you don't know anything about it, because your eyes tell you stories. They make you believe that people exist because you see them. I didn't have that illusion any longer. I was left with another one: that I could see them, if I touched them.

That is why I now call this need an illusion. Once more I am going too quickly; surely too quickly. At age ten, I was still very simple, and if I touched, I saw. But it wasn't true for very long. I was at the edge of the great desert.

What a sad name that is for this phase of life when we become men and women! But there isn't really another. The whole of adolescence, unless you're crude, is nothing but distance and burning. The last time a girl allowed me to touch her I wasn't twelve yet; nor was she. Nevertheless, we hurt one another. Her body was that of a child. We had to interrupt ourselves: there was no longer the resistance of former times; it responded to my touch. It would hurry ahead and it was going to have a soul. It is only during childhood that legs are made for running. A time comes when the merest bit of flesh speaks for the rest, and says as much as the mouth or the eyes. At twelve, a taboo was placed on my fingers.

Society was responsible for it. The French bourgeoisie of thirty years ago did not like the instincts any better than that of 1900. But I'm not going to speak to you about society, because it never explains anything fully. It's one's age that does all the work.

It makes all the feelings and intentions emerge on the surface of the body. I couldn't stretch out my hand any longer without hurting a heart. How could I take hold of a wrist, and go up to the arm? I couldn't really do that without throwing myself totally towards the other, without breathing in a whole being all at once. The universe is as dangerous as a destiny. Every word is destiny, every gesture. At the same time, an awful misunderstanding begins.

At thirteen, at fifteen, we boys, we no longer have the right to touch—and we don't even have the courage to do so. We don't even have the right to look; we just observe out of the corner of our eye, but we talk about it all the time. We talk about the unique subject, and we speak about it so badly! The girls don't know it, don't even suspect it. They would like so much to believe us to be romantic. We are only when we pretend to be, or when we know someone is listening. And the rest of the time, it's an apprenticeship; not of love, but of vanity. It is a question of who will be the cleverest, the most vulgar. It is a question of who will put his hands everywhere first. The hands! Well! the words. It is up to the one who manages the best and the quickest to forget what he feels. Because for boys there's a moment—even if it doesn't last more than a few weeks—when they all know that their bodies are not objects but living beings; and the bodies of girls are other types of beings, still more alive and so fragile that, if one were foolish enough to name all its parts—simply naming them—would break them. It is this soul of the body, this soul on the body that they all wish to forget, almost all of them. It makes them so afraid.

Yes, it frightened me too. But I only had to look as one looks into the sun, holding hands above my eyes in order to see longer and more clearly. What happened to my body related so little to the physical. Very early on I received the grace to understand that sexuality is not a carnal business but a meeting. And if the body is the place of the meeting, then it is not the cause. The meeting takes place elsewhere.

So I started to make love within my soul—my body pushing, interrupting. And I lived solitude with a fury. Solitude has been so hard for me (and it meant so little), that I finished by lifting it into the divine. Without this folly it would have been unbearable. I decreed that a girl's body was an object of religion. I knew it was becoming something totally new, something so full of expectation that it would burst at the slightest touch. I knew that not a single word—and certainly not those of my buddies—could tell me what was happening in this rising of the future and the joy, up to my chest and in my gut. The words of men disgusted me. Not really; because after all I was using them too. But it was just a stupid code, an agitation of little bells against ghosts, a scandalous unreality, a refusal of reality. The reality is that you can't think about the body of a girl unless you are prepared to go to it completely. It is like believing in God; it doesn't allow half measures.

There is that moment of earliest youth (and one has to love it because we still live on it thirty years later) where the whole physical world is brought to such a heat that it evaporates. It is the moment when everything that is visible, everything that has a contour, and to give a name doesn't seem possible, if you learn that you are going to meet a girl and she is going to be a real one, you prefer to run away. And isn't it astonishing that at that moment when the body is nothing more than an absurd piece of baggage, the weight of which irritates, and you wish the body would disappear, is precisely the moment when sexuality settles in us. That is why I say that sexuality does not really belong to the physical. It is a breaking of bounds; it is the soul that is flooding.

During at least three years, possibly five, I stopped loving the concrete. I only accepted it in the form of plants, of nature. Everything which reminded me that human beings are made of flesh and that they can't even speak without the words coming out between their teeth threw me into a sort of of anger.

It is true that I was more isolated than others. Others had their eyes which provided them with sights. I had only my soul, and that meant famine. But did others manage better?

I had to go to the very end, and because the soul devoured the body I had to allow myself to be devoured. I had to accept the horrible pain to see the girls—the other half of me—leave forever. How could I reconstruct the bridge before complete love? And complete love, did that exist for everybody? Was it possible to believe that it which was not there today would fall one day into my life, as simply as a cry that pierces the silence? Was it possible to believe in anything else than hunger?

Hunger, that was real. That was something that permeated me, that allowed me to tolerate my body. Solitude, that was real: my soul reduced to its desire, no longer suffering that I name its desire, was chasing the specific images away—all of them—, vibrating day and night like a wheel.

I wasn't worried about girls any longer. They had become the other sex. They also had for a moment to be all alone and not know that I existed. Waiting was a sign, emptiness was a sign. Waiting and emptiness were more dense than all the rest of the universe. And everything that was dense was beautiful. The fact that I couldn't imagine anything else apart from emptiness, was still another sign, it was a promise.

Today, I say "signs;" then, I said "dreams." I was going to mobilize all the dreams and impose them on life so that finally the doors would break down. Because I could not meet any girls any longer, because even the sound of their voices, that alone, was too much for me, because none of them had a finished air about them, because everything had an incendiary taste, because the slightest details—the way a young woman walked, or her conversation—seemed either too precious to be kept or on the contrary too stupid, I was going to love love. I was going to love it all by myself, far away from the body, far away from people. I was going to love it the way one prays, until it can remold the world.

That is where I had got to one summer evening, when a particular girl—and she was no longer just a sign—came and overtook me. But, you remember, not me alone: but Pierre and me together. The next day (I remember this small detail suddenly), as a fly lit on my arm, I became aware that I liked the fly. The fly and all the other objects of the living world. And the more particular they were, the more they were real again. And the more particular the girl I loved was, the more universal she became. In the meantime, the great image was born.

It was born in the furnace of those lifeless years. I mean those years where the life within me was so total that it could not bear to take any forms, where the whole of the future was contained in my ignorance, where ignorance was a knowing which no experience would ever replace, where I was always right by virtue of forgetting to what I applied my passion, where no one had come yet to say "yea" or "nay" to my faith. For when I loved one girl, I ceased, at least for a time, to love all the girls; I was mistaken, a little mistaken, about all the others. As soon as I preferred her voice to all the other voices, I ceased to hear them. And if one day I loved another, everything would have to start all over again.

You wanted me to talk to you about my hands again. But at that time I didn't have any anymore. Nevertheless, I can see them still: they were not dead; they were only condemned. It is in an attic that I see them again. An attic, because I found one wherever I went. In every house it was the only place that was poor enough to be rich. The book I was reading I let fall on the trunk which served as a table and I was holding my arms dangling on either side of my body with the hands hanging down. I couldn't do anything else with them, except to cross them perhaps—but one doesn't pray all day. Forbidden, they really were. I had no use for them. On whom could I place them? The girl I had loved had never climbed into this attic. Her face filled the small window, her voice trembled against my temples; but even her voice and her face entered, then left, without my being able to do anything about it. This exquisite form that she had was not made of forms. As to touching her, I wouldn't have known how nor would I have wanted to. My hands were only memories. They remembered their innocence. That was years ago. Then they could touch as eyes look: without being seen. And the anguish of such an injustice took hold of me.

Eyes had every right. Even Pierre's could rest wherever they liked. Yet his were of a prudishness that was almost immaterial. Those of my other friends, I knew it well, were constantly marauding. And they did so with impunity. They could get entwined in the locks on the back of the neck, slither around the waist, invade, treat brusquely. Even that: to treat brusquely; to climb under a skirt and be there where the other person should have remained alone. They had a revolting permission. And it cost them nothing, it didn't commit them, because eyes have that detestable power, a power that no other part of the body would ever possess: that of being detached. Eyes, I even knew eyes who took it upon themselves to be ironic. I would like to have seen them be ironic with their hands! A hand which doesn't quite believe what it touches, a hand that gives itself and withdraws immediately, a mocking hand, is the hand of a thief! The hand of a rascal. I, when I touched, I was totally in my fingers. Which part of me could I have held back? To place one's fingers on another human being, it is to precipitate towards him everything one has: one's whole life, one's soul. To place one's fingers is to take. I so much wanted it to have been less serious. But ah! it was serious. Her soul. Even that word was misleading. To extend one's fingers is to extend one's whole body— including one's sexual organ. Rape is inevitable. The shadow grimaces about it in the palms of your hands. And those hands, if you love, you can no longer open them.

You see, in nascent love there is no place for fingers. Otherwise there would have to be a freedom, a childhood which is rejected by the whole of our civilization. Youth at sixteen is an incongruity, it is unhealthy, it is too late, nobody wants it anymore. I too didn't want it any more. But it came back in flashes of lightning, with a longing to touch nevertheless, to ask permission gently, to say that it was without importance and that after the touching one would forget. These longings had to be pushed away, and immediately! They had become ugly.

I was biting my fingers. Why did those animals have eyes, since I could lead them no-where? To touch myself? I did it, but with a sad impatience like a canker under the tongue. After one or two minutes, I stumbled over slippery forms, said and said again, hollow forms. And this hollow was not even the imprint of the world on me. I reflected nothing anymore. The mirror turned. A hundred mirrors, a single image. The despair of the mole. And my fingers hadn't touched anything, nothing at all! One can only touch when one is invited to.

But I'm telling you about my anger. Did I live through it then or is it only today that I am inventing it? Because I had lost my eyes and I no longer had the right to touch, yet in exchange I had received a far more powerful sense: the inner gaze; and I used it when I was sixteen. So? So I suppose I shouldn't think of all that any longer, but I am experiencing it again. I have to be in my attic again and that girl has to come back.

On bad days if I wanted to see her, I would only take hold of the folds of a curtain with my nails scratching it and feel my breath come back to me. The curtain wasn't even outside of myself in the room: it was against my eyes, and soon under my eyelids. It cut the world in two: myself and the others. And I, was only that battle with a curtain. She, I still saw her, but only here and there. Her voice, the memory of her voice, gave me her neck, a shoulder; and the rest of her body would slip from hand to hand between the glances of the others. I had to ask Pierre, to ask him again how she walked, how she stood up. On bad days I couldn't find her joints: the ankles and the knees, the waist, the elbows and the neck. It was the transition from a curve to an angle, the birth of the movements. Immediately afterwards, what I lost was the texture of the skin and the dimming of light which, depending on the moment, rendered it vermillion or crystalline. I only saw welded forms, the smothering drapery of the curtain. If she rang our doorbell unexpectedly and ran across the hall, I heard the clicking sound of her sandals; but it only said sandals. That is when I wanted to touch, at all costs and anywhere: even an object that she carried—her bag, her bracelet. I would not have demanded more. In fact, at such moments, to touch her arm would have shattered me. What I couldn't tolerate any longer, was this fog, the accordion-like folds of this fog.

On good days, on the contrary, everything happened as if I had twenty or a hundred eyes that could touch everywhere. They touched her like very light fingers which can lift, separate, enlarge and press on keys at ever changing distances— those of a keyboard out of which would emerge little rays of light. And nevertheless, on those days, it was not her body that I touched, not the one of which Pierre with his inexhaustible conscientiousness would again and again give me a description; but her other body, the one that was floating around her, the one that she was inhabiting when she was quiet, and of which the gestures of everyday life were only a memory. This second body, I devoured it with my sight. It was above her, behind her. It followed her everywhere. It rose and descended with her voice. But it was far more beautiful, always a little more beautiful than what she said or did. It seemed to be her real house, and I couldn't quite understand any more why she needed to come in through the door, to climb the stairs. Rather more beautiful and a little larger and lighter too; and above all it was the body of another girl. It was really the body of the girl that I loved, so much that I, the only one who kept seeing this other body, was also the only one to know her.

Everybody—and Pierre himself—took her to be a very sweet girl, but capricious and sometimes languishing. It was because they didn't see the other body. There, she had decisiveness, prickles; there, she had weapons. And also a patience, a way of marking time and keeping to it, the bearing of a good soldier. That is how she was in her second body. She was as strong there as she was weak in the one that the others saw.

You might say to yourself: but what joy to be pulled out of the stupidity of appearances! To have the right to look twice, once at the trivial level and then at a more elevated one. How marvelous to be thrown, in spite of oneself, into the invisible! Indeed, it was a kind of happiness. At least it was a perch, and I was trying to hang from it. But I fell down again. The invisible is too difficult. For what we are, it is not secure enough. It tires one like a doubt which could return at any time. There were moments when I would have given all my inner light for one ray of sunshine as others see it. The blurriest half–light would have seemed precious to me. I would have given all those invisible bodies for the hem of her dress or the color of her bodice.

I was never able to rest five minutes, not even the length of a breath, about everyday things, those which resemble others and which we share with everyone, those about which we can speak at any time to anybody without any caution, those which carry common names. And perhaps they're half true, half false; they have no sparkle; but at least we aren't the only ones to be deceived by them. My girl was certainly less beautiful in the eyes of the others who beheld her than in mine. Pierre, who was constantly belaboring the fact, was undoubtedly right, and he believed it—I knew that he believed it. But, even with him, I would so much have liked to tell him certain self-evident things about her. Instead of that, I only had some truths. What could I do with them?

For me, people either lost all outline, gathering themselves into the black plush of a ball of velvet; or else they lit up beyond all human measure; they sparkled with a light which was no longer of this world. And I, between the two of them, where could I stand? For I was neither black, dog-eared and fading, nor transparent and stitched with rays like the king of the legend. Never so small, never so great. I was in love with a girl and my eyes gave me a star. A second body—and that was true, it taught me more about her than the other one; but would there ever be a means for me to know the first one? There would have been my fingers; I thought about them all the time. But nobody invited them. And even if my girl had signaled them one day, what would they have met? It was round about this time that I began to be afraid of bodies.

One could have been frightened of less. Just imagine those transformations which they were all undergoing in my mind. There they all became either more beautiful or more ugly than by nature. They hardly seemed to have any limits: they came out of faces in order to enter into the voices. I saw them right down into the silences, in the echo of a footstep, into the creak of a door, into the swish of a piece of cloth, a drop of water in the courtyard which would recall the imperceptible explosion of saliva at the corner of a mouth, a book which closed at the exact rhythm of a thought. They were clearer still—of that I was certain—and as a result more secret. They never seemed like objects. The way I saw them, I couldn't have moved them. And there was no question of replacing them with others. I only had one wish and one sole right: to speak to them. The joy I anticipated was of addressing myself to each one of them in particular. Oh! If only I could have interrogated them! If only I had been allowed to interrogate the body of my girl! But that couldn't be; I didn't have the eyes that were needed. Mine would have seen too much. She would have judged them to be indiscreet. She couldn't have borne them.

What fatigue! I seem to remember fatigue above all. Not to be able, even for a brief hour, to live in the ordinary. Not to be able to blend two bodies together, even if they resemble one another to the extent of confusion. To be thrown back on the essential as the only nourishment that was allowed. The soul does not always have that appetite.

It too needs short moments of happiness. "At midday, I was able to look at her for at least five minutes without her seeing me. I simply stayed where I was: at the window. She was chatting in the courtyard with her two friends. The girlfriends weren't bad. But if only you could have seen that she of the three was the most beautiful!" "Last night, at a particular moment, I was not sure if she was looking at me. I think she was distracted to the point of not seeing anything. But her eyes were wide open on me, and I did it, you understand: I plunged right into the depths." It was Pierre, not I, who experienced these surprises. He was entitled to supplements. I wasn't jealous. Not at all! Not of Pierre. And then, wasn't he the one who lent me his eyes? But I wondered if I, myself, would ever have any surprises.

I wanted so much to compare, to make mistakes as others do, to know at last all the details of a leg, even if there should be some I would regret. Pierre said that I would be disappointed—yes, even with her. He explained to me that no one was completely beautiful to the eyes, for there's always, here or there, a form that needs correcting; that in a sense, a funny sense, I couldn't even imagine how fortunate I was that I was protected against these wretched plays of light and shade in which the eyes get enmeshed. And this other fact: one always sees badly. You're never placed exactly where you should be. Or everything is in its right place—and that's a miracle, you could at last use your two eyes and see everything; but she knows that you are looking at her, she is embarrassed, then you are embarrassed and don't look at her any longer. Pierre was certain that I would always be happier than he. So, how could I have been jealous of him? One saw from the outside and he was certain not to see clearly. The other saw from within and that too was not enough. And there were days when we would both laugh about it: we were both blind.

There were other days when the inner paradise resembled a junk room, where I only met broken dreams, barbed wire bodies, calls of life, cold as drafts of air, and where, for the first illusion, or any material proof, I would have given all my light. I couldn't stand it any longer, being so deep, so distant, so perfect and so vague in all my visions, so close to the center of myself, of the universe. I wanted to mix myself up with everything, to fragment myself, follow forms until I lost sight of them, to reassure myself that she had straighter knees, less knotty than those of other girls, hips more tender than those of others, but hips. I wanted to compare all the little things among themselves, pass hours doing so. After that, I would know where the essential was; but before . . . before rolling myself in a sea without end of everything that appears and of everything that hides itself, I only had this torrent in my veins and my soul, and for this torrent no bed. My girl, I could not compare her to anything, except the grand image.

But what finally was this image? It was one of a woman: undressed. I don't mean that in the physical sense. A woman stripped of everything that makes her unique, of everything that obliges you to give her a name, of everything that forces you to speak differently to her, to love her differently, to love her alone—and if you don't do it this way, it will no longer be her and she will go away. It was a woman, but I never knew, I never had the means of knowing where I would meet her nor when. She was there in front of me; she appeared in the girl that I loved; it was blinding. And then it was no longer she. I had always known her, I couldn't meet her suddenly. I had known her before I came into this world. I came into this world because of her. So, why should she be someone suddenly? Why this girl and not another? Would I ever know? My image (I had at least to make an hypothesis about it), no girl could ever become it. I had too much life to be alive. How could this flood one day be contained within a single body? She was luminous all over, with luminous fingers, a stomach, a luminous back. But, in reality, was there a body without shadows? Pierre repeated that it wasn't so, and he didn't need to tell me. She ran ahead of me, she never stopped running. As soon as I caught sight of her, I ceased to see her. As soon as I no longer saw her, she reappeared again in my eyes. If I touched a fold of her dress, her dress became a cloud. I couldn't catch up with her. Never.

Sometimes she resembled me. I might have believed that she was me. Sometimes she was so different that I wasn't certain whether I existed on my own account. She was "us," I often said to myself. But who was this "us?" What place did "us" occupy in time?

For others, love was the absolute opposite: it was to love the first one that comes along, or the last one. Yesterday, he didn't know her yet; you wouldn't even have dreamt of knowing her. Or perhaps he had already met her, but had not figured that it would be she. Today, she had said yes, and she had stopped being difficult, she was open to what he wanted (not absolutely everything, but it would come by and by). She swore that she would not look at the other boys anymore, and she stopped; and he, he would only see her; if she saw him thinking of another, she would no longer love him. It was him, it was her. Life stopped. And there they were, loving each other.

It is in these terms that they all spoke about love. Except for Pierre. But Pierre was made of another metal, and he had succumbed to my contagion. Love, for them, was someone. Before, that didn't exist. After, that could be no one else. Or otherwise, they would have been mistaken, they had never loved that one; that hadn't really been love. I had such difficulty in understanding them.

The girl I loved, I had hoped that she was the one, and the only one. I prayed that it might be she. But I swear that

I have never known. She seemed so beautiful as soon as I started to love her, that she must have been Love. But what would prove to me that she would be "my love?" And those two words, "my love," which I heard everywhere, I didn't feel like saying them. They seemed so much like a theft. It seemed as if I had slipped stealthily into the treasure and had snatched a coin. It was as if I had mutilated love.

I seemed to say foolish things. It is not possible that I had never wished to become for her "her love." I wanted that, of course. I wanted only that for three years. But, each time I wanted it, and the more strongly I wanted it, something in me tightened. I was no longer certain that I had the right to be right. I was no longer certain of remaining faithful. There was a wait (one could call it a promise) to which I was lying, I felt it. I loved loving her. It was more important than being loved in return. I liked the movement of love which threw me onto her. I loved what love made of me, as soon as it was so violent; what it made of her, even when she was not aware that I loved her. If finally she had come to share love with me, a frightening happiness would have shaken me, I would have keeled over and rolled for months and months, I would have left my roots. But love, how do I know if it still would have been there?

Ah! If, at eighteen, I had suddenly learned that she also saw the great image; if I had caught her looking on me as a copy—the clearest and the most terrifying; if I could have been certain that she would never have believed that I was hers, nor that she was mine, then perhaps . . . But I learned nothing of that. Before you, I learned it from no one.

To prefer love itself to the love of another being. And yet to love a being only now and then, is so interminably difficult. And to start so early in life! But in fact, has it come to an end? Are we, you and I, today, ready to accomplish this? I mean: without failing, at every moment. Do I love you enough when I pass through you, cherishing all the bedrooms, all the stages? And in the end, do I love you outside of yourself? On your side, are you certain to prefer love to me? I don't mean from time to time and when our bodies and our souls are resting, but when I'm holding you.

You must be right: we shall never have the answer.

5

"If all those good women could hear us talk about them when they are no longer there, I tell you, my brothers: they would be taken by a natural and holy horror; they would take their rosaries and they would run as fast as they could; soon there would be no more room in the convents."

He was right, Cadou. Like the people from his part of the country, he had moments of great eloquence, that is to say, of light. But soon afterwards, he started telling his stories again—and they were thicker than ever.

It is true that for months now we had been in the hole, and for months we hadn't breathed a living perfume, hadn't heard the sound of a woman. Except for the "mice" of the gestapo ("those counterfeits," as Cadou called them). It is true that what we got was the return of the instincts and their display. And, Cadou would surely have added: "All things considered, if one of you can provide me the proof that a child can be made with words, then let him stand up!"

I was ashamed to feel shame. I hadn't known that I was a prude to that extent. I was embarrassed to the point of disgust to find that I was the only one who was so ill at ease. Weren't we among men? Was there any harm in expressing our needs? Weren't mine, in the silence of my youth, weren't they the same as those of Cadou and the two others, exactly the same? It wasn't only that we were deprived of women: we were deprived of everything that was feminine. Between these four walls there was no indulgence, no hope. There wasn't even the slightest trace of patience. There was no hand on our foreheads. Then wasn't it better that this hollow emptiness, so soft and necessary, would rise from our bodies and would lose itself in words? I simply had to get used to it. I would not always be eighteen years of age.

But I was ashamed. I would have liked to know why. It wasn't the words. First of all, there were not more than about a dozen, and I had known them all since the age of ten. I had understood that if there is one domain which challenges language, it is that of sexuality. I knew that no one would be able to say what happens inside when experiencing desire—that the parts of the body, they can't be named—nor the parts of the soul—and everything gets confused, there are no longer any images. I knew that the words came as best they could, and that they are all dull, or hairy, but at least recognizable. Yet I closed my eyes. I closed them so tightly that my eyelids trembled. I was so deeply ashamed.

For myself or for them? One day I would have to decide. They seemed to be happy: they were howling. Their upper bodies were naked, and they were exercising between the door and the window, between the blinking of the peep-hole and the gleam of the unpolished tiles. They were repeating that they were men, and that they would go charge and smash things. They were shaking sleigh bells, hammers and waving flags. They had a little less pain in their bodies. They wouldn't have hurt a fly. Cadou, who was the voice for all the others said it: "Every time that I screw in words, it is always that much spared from bad dreams."

I did not speak as they did. I couldn't do it. Perhaps that was my shame. Perhaps I was dying to imitate them. I tried. I did it. I played like they did, like a Tartarin (a French folk character) on horseback on a puppet. I didn't do so badly. They all thought that I had joined the gang. But I didn't stop being ashamed.

Like all eloquent braggarts, Cadou had his moments of modesty. Sometimes he knew that I was ill at ease, and he, for whom all innocence was a sort of original sin, he would stop short in the middle of his dance and start to dream. No, I assure you: it was not the words.

How much time did we spend every day in prison in thinking about sex? About half the time, roughly. And, some days, when we were gripped by the fear that we would never get out of the clink, more than half of the hours. We thought about it, some by talking about it, others in silence. But what difference did it make? Desire, sex, had become our only weapon. It was the only branch of life that we had to push against the walls and break them down. And even that was threatened by the thin atmosphere of the cells, the humid immobility, the absence, the repetition, the ghostly waiting, and the bromide dumped into the soup—everybody said so. We simply had to continue as best we could. Then one wakes up with words. Words are virile members. I also brandished them. I didn't say they were superfluous.

The shame didn't lie in vulgarity. This vulgarity was a way of unwinding; it lightened the burden. The shame was in the pictures.

For I saw what they saw, Peltier, Cadou and Lefort—and later Greder, after Peltier had been suddenly released, and later still, Thonon, after Cadou had been called away on transport. The narrowness of the cell, its simplicity as a dark room had given me back the strength which many years of study and an active life had eroded: attention. I became as attentive as I had been when I was eight. But, this time, I did not go fishing for marvels; I only brought back rusty bits of iron.

As soon as they started talking "women," I opened my eyes wide. What were they going to show me? But Cadou was bragging, Peltier was singing his broad jokes, Lefort was sniffling about his poor fate between two swear words. Already I was no longer listening to them: I was looking for forms. I was looking for a woman—any one—a face. There was never a face. I looked more closely: surely there would be a mouth reaching out, arms that laugh. At least there would be thighs and hips! I couldn't believe my eyes: there were no women: there were only tools. For hours, in the middle of this cell on a spree, I saw only pliers and nails, ladles and pots, balloons, bags, rope. And I who imagined them. It was they who hit against them, filled them, allowed them to drain drop by drop. They called that love; and they weren't joking. It wasn't even repugnant. All those gals they paraded, every day the same ones, were reduced to nothing. Reduced to vises and cuts. The work of a mechanic. Not a living form, not even the slightest beginning of one. If I was ashamed, it was because of this poverty. It weighed on my head, it blocked my senses. If only they had played with marionettes! If they had given them arms and legs! Only Cadou, sometimes, because of all this bawdiness and gaiety or perhaps because of this exaggerated sense of glory which, at times, made him almost handsome, would make appear a piece of cloth, a bit of skin. But, as soon as he got there and we were about to see a girl, he would stop, his voice humid, and I knew that within five minutes, all bawdiness sent to the doghouse, he would be talking to us either about his mother or about his little girl who was only three years of age.

You cannot imagine what I would have given for the solution to the enigma. Because after all, if they could repeat again and again for weeks their sagas of tools and butts without even once a real gesture, an incarnated creature jumping into my eyes, was it because they were protecting themselves, or because they didn't dare? Nevertheless, if I had told them, "Dare, for God's sake!", they would have laughed in my face. It was really a question of daring! In this domain of men they were kings; they all believed it. And if I was the young fellow with a virgin soul; they would certainly have let me know it.

For the past ten years, since my accident, I had lived in a world where every word was a being, where every being had a form, where every color expressed a thought, where every thought met a soul, where every spark of love lit up eyes, a waist. I came to ask myself if that world was not an erroneous one, if my images were those of men. They, after all, did not have any images, or hardened ones that clacked like locks. Strangely, when finally they spoke about other things—their dogs, their towns, their professions, their childhood— lines formed themselves, a frame, a scent. There were even characters. It was love, love only, which made them as small as moles. It was the love of the body, the love one expresses with the body. There, everything went wrong, it all dissolved in fat or in sawdust. But then, why?

They didn't dare—I always came back to my hypothesis—and Cadou even less than the others, although he was the most sonorous. Every evening, after the lights went out, while Lefort or Peltier were making the last movements of their arms and jaws which preceded sleep (in five minutes they would be snoring), I would turn towards Cadou and his tensed muscles. Even while resting, this man had muscles. First we would talk. We would whisper so as to create the impression of being alone. He would question me; I would explain. He also responded. He was an honest fellow and had an inquisitive spirit. I think he would have replied to all my questions if only I had put them to him. Then after a while, every evening, he stopped responding. It wasn't that he was sleeping (like me, he still needed a couple of hours before sinking): it was, on the contrary, that he woke up. And for him, waking up was slow. He moved his body in supple motions from one side to the other, folded and unfolded it in gymnastic movements in which a dream might have inserted itself. I listened so acutely that my own breathing was suspended, and at times I had to catch it again. I listened to him imagining; I listened to him seeing. Now that he no longer spoke, Cadou must have been seeing. He was not a brute; he had a heart, a presence to beings—during the daytime vain, but reconciled at night; surely he must have seen someone.

His body was no longer alone. I could hear that. I could hear him making room, withdrawing a little here, covering an empty space there. On the straw bed, his gymnastics took place at such intervals and with such care that it was clear to me: he was taking someone else into consideration. I was so joyful to have discovered this that learning more about it would not have interested me much more. Perhaps it was his wife that he was seeing—the mother of his little girl, as he said during the daytime. Perhaps it was another woman, or maybe some others. It didn't really concern me. The essential thing was that instead of a whole display he had someone in his eyes. From time to time he sighed briefly. Never on these occasions, did a heavier sound escape him—him, the appointed tenor for the song "The Artilleryman of Metz." The damned irreverent devil had become light.

What he saw, I never knew; and how would I have asked him? But, one night, I asked him whether he saw anything, and he did not hesitate: "Do I see them? And how!" Nevertheless, by the tone of his voice, I felt that for him it was too difficult, that he would have liked to renounce it, that he could not, that there was something in the images of those girls which mocked your imagination, that they were all, all the time, the same and that they would drive you crazy. What needed to be found was precisely the unfindable thing: the curve of the breast which only existed in this one, the folds of the body which would have had her voice.

And the next morning, during the obscenities shared while we had coffee at seven o'clock, I said to myself that I must have made a mistake, that his "and how" had only been one of those complicities that are needed between men, one more. All together, I imagined what he saw, but I never saw it. Here again, what was happening in his head was not strong enough to run, real and clearly drawn, from his straw bed to mine. Nevertheless, if it had been enough for a man to be silent in order to see, what a marvel! What a deliverance, if words were our only enemies! Perhaps the rudeness of Cadou was nothing but a disguise, a roll on the big drum, in order to cover up the little voice of a heart that was too young. But I tell you, that man had a heart.

All of them in the cell had heart. Each one his share. And that was what made them bearable. But each time their hearts unrestrained turned to women, they would cease to talk. They would enter into a silence without description, and where their bodies (I would catch that departure on a wing) had almost completely disappeared. You would have thought that they couldn't both live and feel at one and the same time. To both desire and love was totally out of the question. There was no malice; not within them. They were quite ordinary guys. In Cadou, who was perhaps not quite ordinary, there was even a certain delicacy. But in all three, there was the same misery: either they delved into their bodies and it was like the din of drinking songs; or else they took refuge in their souls, and then it was a two hours' silence. What am I saying silence! If it had only been that! It was the night of the images; it was the lamp that flickers and is about to go out. At last I began to believe it: for them, for myself, the difficulty was not being imprisoned and holding on; it was not waking up every morning to the same guard rattling his keys in the lock and the three unchanged mugs of my comrades. It was having a body and a soul that were living together, and which one didn't know how to use.

For I was unable to see more clearly what went on in them when it was "feelings time" (and for me it was a new sorrow) than I could when they were singing guard house songs. Nevertheless, in prison, feelings came from such grave and violent causes that one could only take them to be real. Lefort had actually witnessed his wife being arrested at the same time as he was. He knew that she was on the same floor as we were, thirty cells away in the womens' section. He could not be more certain of her fate than he was of his own. Peltier asked himself where his children and their mother might have sought refuge after his arrest. He had left so little money; and there were hardly any relatives. And then for everyone, there were the walls. If you haven't been a prisoner, you can't imagine what those four walls are like. They cut off all your ties. They even cut into your memory. They squash you with an idea heavier than yourself, against which you have no more heart: even if a miracle happens, even if I'm liberated, I will no longer find anybody; or, if I find them again, they will not be as they were before; on the other side time does not march as it does here; I will have lived one year, they will have lived ten; nobody will recognize me . . . I shared the same feelings with them. At least there we were one. The window pane between us was at last going to be washed clean.

Alas, it was more smeared. You would have said a dirty blue—(was that ridiculous from where we were)—a passive defense with its glass windows. I knew it straight away when one of them was suddenly dreaming of his little girl in the silence of tears which don't quite come. But in the space in front of him, in the space where he was looking for her, there was no child. He held her close, however; he caressed her, but like a woman. And if it was the suddenly complete absence of his wife which gnawed at him, a frantic gentleness and rocking would take hold of him. She would take on the face of a little girl—and the body.

At true moments of emotion, there was a confusion which went so far that people were completely erased. Mother, spouse, daughter, they were all one. It was a blanket pulled up over the eyes. They muffled up in order not to see anything anymore. What I saw was the coming and going of their clenched fingers, especially those of Lefort (he was constantly scratching his straw bedding), in the direction of an obscure zone, at the very bottom of his pain, where no one would be any different from anyone else (not even he himself from those whom he loved), where there was no longer a name to shout, where there would be no time that passes, and could no longer pass, where the future would be like the time before life: an absence, one long absence.

I didn't blame Lefort, nor his way of scratching the canvas which served him as a bed. His flight, I experienced it too. When my heart was pained, it galloped like his towards the black center, towards the germ of all childhood. And there I could have wept, because there was nothing. There wasn't anyone any longer, neither body nor soul. How have we been made then, to no longer see anything as soon as we suffered?

Nevertheless, feelings are beautiful. They have something which enables one to forgive. To my neighbors, they gave back the gesture of humanity. And then, they had a secret taste and a kind of soft light: that of modesty. After all, I wasn't going to regret the red and the black of their songs!

Modesty. At that time, I liked it. I liked its trembling and its morning color with which it covered everything. I thought it was a virtue. I wanted to practice it myself, to be capable of it more often, to make it stand guard over all my dreams, to mix it with love as in a marriage that would be celebrated day and night. I thought that it protected love. Modesty, I loved it like a voice, like a tone. I needed it because instead of throwing my images into a whirlwind and giving them over to currents of thickness, it made them run and fly, untying them. In my comrades, I didn't recognize it.

Modesty, immodesty, it all seemed the same. Towards the end of the year, Mollien had replaced Cadou. And this newcomer was really not like the others. He had manners, a certain frowning reserve, which forbade him a dormitory mentality, which prevented him from uttering a single unsuitable word. He was tall, twenty-eight, and spoke like someone who manicures his nails; he heralded another world. All this business of decency. Did it go back to education? I started studying Mollien.

In fact, in the course of a month, not a single word which could relate to sexual things came out of his mouth. It was almost a relief. But, quite quickly I noticed something else: he had an inclination. And this inclination, in spite of his perfect diction, and his choice of words—or perhaps because of both—daily took an ever increasing place in the cell; he obstructed everything. Mollien turned his tongue seven times in his mouth, but not in order to avoid dirtying anything: he did it in order to let go of the word or the story which was pressing in from all sides. And his stories were all eschatological.

Some of the others had also had this quality, but rarely in such an exclusive manner. His were monochrome, insistent, and distinguished. And from their distinction they drew a pompous absurdity, such an indiscreet racket, that not only I, but the others too, we finally stopped him: "Shut your trap, we've heard you already." Had their raunchiness been less detestable? It's funny: I had never asked the others to shut up.

You can imagine my confusion. Or perhaps in all this I was simply the victim of my own lack of experience, and this scandal of rudeness would one day appear to me as a simple childish unhappiness. But would that day ever come? Because this time, I was called for transport. It was no longer jail: it was deportation, or perhaps I belonged to a different race from all the others (but what an unbearable idea!) since for me, where there was no nobility, there was no love. And by nobility I meant something specific: love, from the first emotions—those to which one doesn't give a name yet—to the complete and shared gestures, for me it was like breathing. Like breathing when you ascend a mountain road, and then suddenly the heavier parts of your body dissolve, and in your lungs you only have this fresh sting, the intake of air in its native state, and even your thoughts themselves have no more mud. For me love was beautiful, like sight, breath, blood. I never felt that I wanted to make it heavy. To make of it a secretion, they—the others—, that tempted them; they didn't resist it. Secretion, excretion, one might have thought that they were emptying themselves. I did not understand. Or rather, would I, engaged in the practice of love as many men ended up doing, more or less every day, more or less in the same way, discover in my turn this sadness?

No. All those fellows had lied. Not once, after all, had I felt that their stories about love were true. They were not stories about love, but about vanity. You simply had to look at them: their vanity became inflated like a sexual organ, became their sexual organ. And what better way to boast of the simplest of acts than by shaking it like a dirty poster? Not one among them had spoken to me during the last six months of a single real woman, a single real man. They all said, "I"— I have done this, I have seen that—out of habit, laziness. What they had seen, and truly done in their life, their vanity—always vanity—never would have allowed them to say. In the realm of love, it is fatal: everybody lies. I had also lied, because I had not had the courage to confess, to intimate even that I was a virgin, like a newly minted coin. Why hadn't I had this courage?

Once again hope took hold of me. During the deportation I would learn something else. All this misery was due to being imprisoned. Could a cell be a good theater for life? Four of us sniffing our twenty-five cubic yards of dead air, having under our eyes day and night only one object: the latrine; incapable of sparing each other a single noise of our bodies; forced every time to collapse when we had no strength left and to do it in public; forced also to reveal whatever we had to hide. How could we be truthful! It seemed to be necessary not to be truthful in order to hold out. An intimate truth, but that would have been the last garment torn away, and the wound would have been immediately visible. Why didn't I think of it! There was no room for confidences in prison.

But in the camp, were there any? I told you often: there were thousands, and as true as humans beings can be true. It's because there we were no longer under the false protection of the walls. Prison was like military service, a sort of quarantine. Certainly death threatened us there as much as in the camps, but we didn't see it. In order to meet it, the door, another door, ten doors would have had to open. In the camp, death was right there. It was there at every minute and in all its forms. It could have been a shot, the stab of a knife, the blow of a pick, dysentery, famine. It could have come from the SS; it could have come from the comrades. It made all of us beings without a future, thus without play acting. And the men talked.

They spoke of their women. They didn't even hide their first names any more. Whether they had been wives, mistresses, or harlots, whether they had had them or missed them, why wouldn't they say who and how they were, because in any case they were dead. The women were not dead, of course. They had stayed on the side of the living, and the men saw themselves dying. But that, they would never have said; they couldn't have done so without running the risk of advancing their death by an hour or by a day. That is why they were always talking about their women, and not of themselves as in the past tense. And there, there were no more secrets. They all behaved as if Josette, Maude, or Madeleine of whom they were telling me would never cross my path. Never. Surely no more than they would. Even less, that's for sure. It was neither fatalism nor despair; it was simply like that. It was simply a way of looking at life a little obliquely, of looking at it from more distance, not mixing it with the present, and not asking oneself about its return. To forget death, you understand, supposing its reality, but without imagining it. They talked to me for hours about their women, and they hardly hesitated anymore; they didn't choose their words. They didn't even boast anymore, except some who suffered from the sickness of lying, and even they at last admitted: "Everything that I've told you, it's just rubbish, but it does me good." All crudity had gone. Where there was no modesty, how could one be vulgar?

As a matter of fact, yes: they still boasted a little, especially when they spoke for a long time. But then there was a little cracking in their voice which said: If I had known, I would have done it this way. They were not glorious as far as love was concerned. Suddenly they saw what they had missed.

In the best of cases, for a month or a year, they had stuffed themselves. They admitted it: stuffed themselves. It was before marriage, or after the honeymoon, or on the occasion of some brief intimacy. It had perhaps been a matter of a few extra mouthfuls. The rest of the time, it had become a habit. When you have a habit, you're content, but don't know with what. She is still your wife, but she could as well have been someone else's. That confession, I have not heard it ten times but a hundred. I heard almost only that. Finally I knew it by heart, that little laugh and the sadness. I could have done it in their stead and saved them the humiliation, or rather the humility. Because they were not proud. None of them really was. There were no more women, and perhaps there never would be any more, and at this instant when it became urgent for them to find them all, to find one, an image could hardly arise. Memories, yes; but not an image. Imageless memories, in other words, regrets. They had not realized to what extent love is precious and that there is simply no greater happiness in life (or rather life itself). But what would life be if one found it again and there was no love? They all believed—yes, almost all of them—that after pleasure love was finished and that it had to be replaced immediately by something else: money, kids, honors, meals, other women. They all wanted to start again. "If I come back, I will start from scratch . . ." But when they said this sentence, they weren't thinking of their trades, nor of their fortune, nor of all the deeds that had made the story of their lives: they were thinking of love. Love, which each one in his own way, had not seen.

Each one in his own way. I really have the right to say that, because I learned it day by day from the time that I became a public writer. You remember: it was between the arrival in the camp and the landing of the Allies in Normandy. During this period, the SS allowed us to send one postcard per month to our families. But this postcard had to be couched in German so that the censorship could read it, and I was one of the ones who knew German best. For weeks on end, I translated messages from seven o'clock in the morning until ten o'clock at night, with interruption only for soup and roll call. They all lined up. I spoke to their wives by way of their dictation, giving the words one after another to a fellow prisoner who knew enough German to spell correctly, but not enough to translate. And practically all of them asked me to sit between them as they dictated and the fellow who wrote, so that I would be the only one to hear the letter in French as they were giving it.

The letter! What a great word! Because these postcards all said the same thing: "I'm in good spirits. Send me anything that you can find that is sweet, especially honey and sweet spice cake . . . " But there was also the name at the top of the card. "My treasure, my love" or "My darling Mimi." There were also the last words. Most of them didn't want those to be known. Inevitably I would know them. But I would not lay my eyes on them. Of that at least they were sure. Naturally it was only an illusion. You can imagine that the fellow who was writing, he too heard everything. In any case, he heard my translation. But they were keen on this pretended distance. They needed a veil or a rag between the words they were going to say and the one to whom they were going to say them.

Hundreds of men passed through my ears. Most of them sat down on a bench next to me and would lean against my temple. They didn't know what to do with their hands. They would whisper, "For a while send some meat or canned fish." But some stood up (about one in every five). They were the ones who would not have envisaged speaking to their wives privately. There were even some who would recite. Or, upright and resolved to say everything in public, suddenly they were caught by fear, and I had to tell them: "Take your hand from in front of your mouth! I can't hear you any more." They had not realized what they were doing.

Seated or standing up, they said nothing. It was not the content of their postcards which ever taught me anything. But I listened to each one in the depth of my being, I rose towards them reaching out with my heart. It was not curiosity, not that alone: I was indefatigably caught by tenderness. I received each of these men (and this had been given to me without my being able to do anything about it) at that moment when they were contemplating the being on earth to whom they were the closest. To that woman he was going to say everything and nothing, because of the censorship, because of the German, because of me and the fellow who put it down in dictation, because of life in the camp, because of life outside the camp, because of the danger, and the words which are not just things, and the names which are not simply people, because of the silence which one has not learned to break. Finally because of the love which is far away, too far away.

But, once their postcard had been translated and sent off, a lot of them would return to me. Having my professional integrity, I would never ask any questions. I really had no need to. "I think that I have found what I should have said." And another, "Did you notice that I was not writing to the real one?" They almost always forgot me. And if at that time I would have had to translate, I could not have done it, because none of their sentences came to a proper end, because instead of looking for words they were seeing. They finally began to see. And when it was no longer a matter of talking and of writing they would find the face—her eyes as they were upon waking—and sometimes, rarely, suddenly: more. Ten seconds later they would speak again. However usually that would stop at the face and the hands, at the very most at the shoulders. Beyond that they were disgusted: it was a woman, but it was no longer she. All women are alike, and that is terrible. Thinking about intimacy! Intimacy is a mass. What they found most easily were the things that concerned them very little: her clothes—those which she wore on a particular day. It is amazing how many descriptions of womens' suits and shoes I heard! Or rather, renounce the details and search for the feelings. They tried. But, as soon as they were moved, they complained again because she had completely disappeared. Erased. They wondered if she had ever been more than a dream. They suffered. There was no way of being there.

Among many others, I remember Menissier. I don't think I ever told you about him. He was a man without any fuss. He must have been thirty-five; he was a civil servant in Moulins; he had been married for ten years and had two children. Usually he spoke very little. I think that no one really knew him. He was an honest man in everything. He had done everything with honesty, including the Resistance. His first postcard gone, he was one of the first who came back to see me. Could he allow himself to talk to me of his wife? Was I certain that it wouldn't bother me? I don't quite remember how in those days I tried to reassure people; but I did apparently reassure them.

He told me where he had met his wife, who her parents were, what she had studied and how he and she had passed their evenings, their Sundays, how they separated their life in two parts—the worries and the dreams—and how surprised they were, both of them, that in the course of time they still loved one another, a little more every day perhaps. In fact I had in front of me one of these men (there weren't ten like him among hundreds) who was proud to love his wife with real love. I thought, to begin with, that this was what he wanted to confide to me. But there was something more. And for this he needed a second permission from me: "Would it bother you, Sir (he was always formal with me), if I thought of her aloud?" He meant: as if I were not there. In this man without visible glory, excessively discreet, a strange lyricism was hiding, a sort of call which would oblige him to imagine in order to live.

He was in the process of losing his wife. He pointed out that it was the case for all the others as well, but that most of them didn't seem to worry about it. The days and the nights passed by and her image disappeared. For a number of weeks now he didn't hear her voice anymore, and it was even longer since he had lost her scent. Now, in turn, the forms too were disappearing. He wouldn't have known how to draw her anymore. Or rather, he saw the way she was when she was a young girl or, more often still, how she was when she was expecting the little ones. It wasn't quite his wife. He wanted to see her when she was his wife. He wanted me to listen: "Tell me, can you feel it! Can you?"

I felt that he loved her, that he had loved her, that he wanted to have loved her more, that as he loved her, he wanted to have known that he loved her. His tenderness was a great and rare success, but as if built on a failure. He came back to it. "Why do I see her so well when she was pregnant?" It was in love that he wished to find her again. If the words had been embarrassing him, perhaps I could help him: "You're not at all forced to tell me everything, you know." But I knew that it didn't matter to him to tell me everything, if only he had been able to tell me, if only he could have seen. He tried to bring back the words she had said to him at the moment of falling asleep. But those, too, he had lost. He tried to forget that she had a body; he didn't take it into account for a moment, in order to see what might happen. It was better, a little better; it seemed as if she were drawing closer to him. She had such a good heart for the little ones, for him; she was so thoughtful. But the misery returned: a woman is not a soul,—what good does it do you to dream of an idea! Her body, he had not known it. It didn't make sense; it was exasperating; he could have wept: he had never known where that body was, had never held it, had held the body of another, of all the others but not hers. Where did that come from? Was he going mad? Would all men have the same experience, if they would question themselves as he did? He wanted me to answer him, and he was certain that I would know. Me, to answer him! "But after all, you remember her when she was a young girl . . ." I don't remember having continued.

It didn't prevent him from coming back to see me every few days. How he must have loved her, that woman, to be so little weary! He never saw her any more clearly except for a second or two, when he was no longer searching. At least, throughout this sad and nuptial wave, Menissier remained modest—far more modest, really, than Lefort or Cadou had been in our cell. Nevertheless, without being able to explain it, I said to myself that I was certain this modesty and that immodesty were one and the same thing.

But, in that case, which was which? Do you know that this question troubled me for years? On one side, I had Lefort standing in the middle of the cell and mimicking with his thumbs and index finger one of those fiestas. It was a night not like the others. There had been about fifteen guys and girls. They were all very drunk. The only corner which was a little darker was the stairway. That was where the two of them went. He couldn't have even said with which one. And, how could he describe the way she was holding on to the banister, while he was working on her from the step below. On the other side, I had Menissier, seated, his hands folded and saying softly that when he looked at his wife, in the evening as she was getting ready for bed, at the moment when she slipped her dress above her head, he felt like pulling on it and bringing it back to her knees so that she might come and sit next to him (not facing him, not immediately), because this suddenly discovered intimacy, he felt, it would have been too much for him. Didn't I have two worlds there? How could I have believed that all this was one and the same world? Didn't Lefort forget his soul on the stairway? Whereas Menissier. . .

Well, with Menissier, it was the same thing. I listened to both of them with the same embarrassment. And this embarrassment, it wasn't just for a trifle—it was the embarrassment of listening to men who spoke to me too closely. It was love called into question. Completely. With, at the end, this question: can it exist? Are there cases where it exists? Are there men who, having started it, completed it? Is there a way of having both a body and a soul together? Must the one be thrown into the thorns so that the other might elevate itself? To elevate! This dimension wasn't even an answer. Was it essential for the one to die so that the other might live?

You see, with Menissier and Lefort, it was the same thing. Neither one could make the transition. The one because of the noise, the other on tiptoe. But neither the one nor the other was able to pass. They were not able to go from the body to the soul, nor were they able to go from the soul to the body. They were on horseback on their instincts—or on their dreams—like men who don't know how to ride. They didn't like their instincts, and they didn't like their dreams. But, what was it that they loved and whom could they love? Both of them embarrassed me, and both of them were painful to me. I was unable to talk about love anymore. Would I one day be the only one for whom love was joyful? That idea was inept. Nevertheless, I had it. At this moment in my life, I was incapable of not having it. Fear of being like the others precipitated me into an illness more serious than all those threatening me in the concentration camp.

When I came back from Germany, I wasn't a man; I was someone who had been resurrected. Others who returned were all like me. But I would have surprised people if I had told them what constituted resurrection for me: swearing never to have a body again without a soul nor a soul without a body. And as for the means of accomplishing this, the whole of humanity, all those thousands of cases, did not tell me how to do it. Do you and I understand them better today? Have we learned about them, from each other? Surely, a little. I would not love you as I do, if we had not made a beginning.

6

But you see, over this there hangs a secret. And it's a secret that is heavy. It's a silence at least, a great silence, and I have never heard a man who broke it completely. It is something that even women do not wish to know. Usually they do not wish to. Then, do you want to?

Well, immediately. We cease to love you as soon as we have loved you. It's not even delayed by a minute. And that is why it's frightening to say it. Even I am afraid. It is at that precise moment, when desire dies. Is love nothing more than that? You must admit: one might indeed be frightened.

In a man, love does not survive beyond desire. They all say to themselves: what! It is already finished! It is finished . . . A few moments earlier, he could see only her: she was immense under their weight; she was immense, stretched out, and curled up, yet so small; she was the unique road; she was the run, the breath, the gallop, and the bursting. She was their only treasure in the world, the only totality. She was complete and simple and close and different—oh, so different as to be out of sight. She was loved. But it is already finished. Their bodies know it, and there is nothing there to replace their bodies. They all search a little, and search they must. The body is all that remains.

Yes! There is gratitude. But, what shall we do with it? Where shall we put it? Gratitude, it is only a feeling. A feeling that never quite has the power of something alive. Gratitude is vague like shame, vaguer still. It will keep us together, for better or for worse for a few hours. Thanks to gratitude we are able to live together as a married couple. Married, there you have it . . . But we weren't promised marriage: we were promised love!

For you, on the contrary, everything begins, and we know that. Even the most obtuse of men know that. Your desire has taken hold of you before we are aware of ours. You hardly had the courage to tell us: we would not have believed it yet. Well before us, and it lasts well after us. Every woman, who is truly a woman, is a marvel after love. It doesn't even depend on what she ordinarily is in life. It certainly doesn't depend on what she thinks. She is a marvel because for her everything now begins. She has received from us everything that we held until that moment of available life; she has not given anything yet herself, nothing really. Her hour will come; it's coming, and it will be long. We are no longer astonishing; she is all surprise. We have withdrawn, we are returned to ourselves again. She becomes change, she becomes everything of which the universe is capable.

I am not necessarily thinking of the child. The child that is the miracle that is added to the wonder. A woman might know that she has not conceived—at least not that time—and nevertheless, she will leave. You all leave. You are what you were before love, but with this addition which we no longer have. Did we give you that? Is it our love, that which we had of love, which has been passed into you? Could pleasure be that, at least that: a heritage? You are so beautiful when you are no longer making love! You are so much more beautiful than we are! What is a man thinking of at that moment when you think he is happier than ever—and who knows! Happier perhaps than yourselves? At that moment when his head sinks into your hair on the tenderness of your shoulder? Have you asked yourself that? He seems to be sleeping. He is going to sleep. But where is he? This hand which a few moments ago held him by the waist and helped him to throw himself to the very depth of your being, does he still feel this hand? You feel it now. The hand that rises in circles from your belly to your heart, closes your eyes. It is that hand that will later on open them again. As for him, he has thrown himself aside on the bank . . . But he is happy! You are quite certain that he is happy. I didn't say that he wasn't. Only desire is not happiness: it is much harder than happiness. And he no longer has any desire. He is satisfied to the very roots of happiness until the next time. He is disappointed.

Do you know what it is for a man to desire? It doesn't at all resemble hunger or thirst: it is far more fragile. For a man the last time might indeed have been the last. How can he know? His health, his youth, nothing gives him any certitude. Desire is every time a minor resurrection. Can you imagine then, what men expect from it?

Everything really. For them, making love is the supreme act; the act that is going to give them everything. By making love, they will find love; that is what they say to themselves. But it is so difficult! For when they desire, they do not love, they do not love you: they love themselves. It is not quite their fault. Nature herself has provided this constriction.

Every man as he penetrates into a woman is so proud! He cannot help it: he is proud. His sexual organ is fully his own: no one can take it away; he fills the space fully; at least for a moment. What he has that is most particular in his body, what is most personal is there, and it grows with every movement, it does not cease to grow. It is not his organ which is working in that woman: it's the whole of him. It is his Self that triumphs. He doesn't call it that, but that is really it. It is the first victory that he has over another. It is the first occupation. Life has found an arm. Courage is easy; there is not even any courage left. There is no need to dream any longer, to dream of what one would be if one were oneself. It is while making love that a man dreams least of all.

At the final point of his gesture, there is the reward. He knows it. He knows that he will have it. But during those last moments he is so much himself that he forgets with whom he is. He utters the name of the woman but he hardly seems to recognize it. It is the name of a hostage, it's the name of the proof. At the moment of orgasm a man has never been so great. Nor so alone, not to this extent. It would be so good for you to know this!

But you should also know that he does not want this solitude, that he came to you in order to get rid of it. But what of it! Man's desire, and his pleasure, is such a deeply acute movement of the flesh, it is so completely a call on all the forces which have built up and destroyed his body that the accident occurs: when he has given his seed, he is nothing anymore, he could not hold back. And you, you are intact.

He believed that he would take everything: he has given everything. How can men still speak of possession? He is sent back to solitude and he wants it less than ever, because he was about to lose it. When he was pounding the depth of your being, for him it was no longer a point in your body, but the doorway. He was about to pass through. He was finally going to enter into someone who was not him. He was finally going to love. His pleasure (yes! even his pleasure) proclaimed it to him. At the second when he was the strongest, he would renounce everything. Then why is what happens so very different? And now you think that he is asleep? . . . Perhaps his body is dozing. But everything else—his plans, his memories, and this interminable waiting that one calls the soul—tells itself: you will have to start again. Making love for a man is bizarre: it is a promise that is not well kept.

Well, as for me, I don't want any of this sadness! I know it's universal. Men have made proverbs out of it. They've made a fatality of it. They are satisfied with it. I've known about it too, as they have. I've known this failure which is so much like anger (anger at the moment when one would wish to love most). But I don't want any of it. I want to understand.

And the normal explanations don't work. The man would have overspent himself . . . He would be the victim of a fluid effusion. But what is it after all, this momentary lowering of the vital current in the face of all this voluptuousness, of this victory that has been given to him? Why doesn't he live this fall as abandon? Why would abandon not be joyful? They say also that this sadness may be due to the slow nature of woman and the hurried nature of man. It may be due to a loss of rhythm, of not being able to create one rhythm together. I don't believe that.

I was talking to you about anger. It reminded me of a young fellow I came across once. He couldn't cope anymore. He was disgusted. He wanted to give up making love, although he was terribly in love. He was afraid of reaching a point where he would hate the body—his own, but hers also. And why? It was that, after making love, every time, he was gripped by fury. "Without reason. On the contrary! Because I love that girl!" Without reason, but with the force which touches on contempt.

I questioned him: why contempt? He had not been brought up in the church. Could it have been shame? He laughed at this idea. No: it was something far more serious, and which did not come from others, but from him alone. While he was involved in the movements of making love, he knew what power was. That is what troubled him. He experienced an inflation of his whole being which, at once, was going to sweep away everything in him that hesitated, everything that was not finished. He said, "I am complete. I am going to be complete." And as he was a sensitive person, he told himself a wonderful story. "I don't know how to love this girl properly. Fundamentally, I do not love her as I love her. But now in a moment I will be able to . . . When all this confusion of weakness has gone, love will be whole."

Each time, he was sure of it. And at the last movement of love, bang, the bolt fell again. Then there was anger.

You see, I don't know why people seek the home of the Self in distant places; it lies in the sexual organs. Perhaps it isn't made to remain there; however, it makes a stop there. When a man is making love, his whole personality does it; too bad if it is insignificant, but it is still there. For a man to have an erection is to learn that he exists. It represents the greatest concentration of himself, that sums him up. We never think about it—women forget it as soon as they can—because we have the bad habit of considering love to be an instinct. Love is only an instinct in its root; all the rest of it is adventure. Love is the greatest attempt at change which humanity knows to this day.

I maintain that only those who are sick and brutal ignore this steam that surrounds the gestures between a man and a woman. A steam . . . How should I put it? Everything that they do is matter, of course. In fact, it is closer to matter than anything else, even than breathing itself. But, however, it is made to suppress it. No! Not to suppress it, but to go through it. In love we are seeking, that's all we are doing. That is why we never cease repeating the same gestures, like children. We don't fear life any longer, not as much as before. It is that unique moment where consciousness and life, these two enemies, find the strength to take a few steps together. It is the moment where what I am, suddenly augmented, until it becomes tangible, is about to meet its resolution: the being of the other, finally. Or the opposite, but it tells the same truth: that is where I will be so much myself, that is where she will be so much herself, that we have no longer any need to exist separately. No need to attack and to defend ourselves, or to continually unravel another mystery, and night after night, to pierce, and to seduce and to be caught. The war has come to an end. Love is no longer an instinct, not today anymore. And, if it is still one, it must come to an end.

But I would do better for the moment to return to our young fellow and his anger. Because he also said that desire in man is of the essence of fire. A solidified flame. Beautiful like the flame, and as clean. As if everything that is burning and dry in the world were about to speak. It traces frontiers as clearly as in a luminous drawing: there is his body, and there is her body; and if they are engaged in one another, yet they do not mix. An incredible hope took hold of him: that it would be like that to the end, that he would always be the man and never anything else, and she the woman. It was then at the very moment of the highest flame that the horrible metamorphosis was taking place: the fire was changing into water. Joy was leaving him. He no longer liked nature. His body had done something different from his will. He had been cheated, soaked into a confusion of all the borders between her and him. Dissolved in laziness, indeterminate as on the first day, furious, beaten. He was no longer a man. I listened to him. There was no doubt that for him it was a defeat, and a dangerous one at that. I tried to tell him: "But this water which bothers you has only the appearance of water. It is alive." But he didn't want to know anything about it. He was angry.

That anger, I am not saying that every man experiences it. For my part, I have never felt it. But I understand it. The rising of the sperm at the summit of this straight up fire that is desire, is in fact quite a surprise. That is precisely a metamorphosis. There at least, he was right. It is like the sign that one has to make of love something other than an affirmation. And that he didn't want to admit. It is truly the moment where man and woman meet one another, the first meeting. Not only because conception can now take place, but above all, because this sudden effusion is a reminder: man and woman are of the same essence. They both belong to the sphere of moisture. They are matter that is being born.

I so much wanted this fellow to let go of his anger; it didn't teach him anything. Once or twice I was about to tell him that his experience was not true (but he believed it to be so true!) that he confused everything, taking his ego for his Self. And the ego needs to be alone, to impose itself whatever happens, to be in the right, even when there is very little ground for it. But the Self never stops at any borders. It is all the stronger as it is involved in exchanges. And this Self, which mattered so much to him (and mine was just as precious to me), what proved to him that it was not more true, complete, and radiating at that moment when, in the animated secret, without boundaries, of both their bodies, it had left the straight and narrow to expand? But I didn't tell him anything, because he thought he was angry. I knew well that he was afraid.

Besides, during the minutes which follow the greatest pleasure, we are all of us afraid, whoever we are. Think about it! Who is the man who dares speak of this capital experience, even to the woman he loves? He has experienced it in her, through her. They could not have had anything together that is more intimate nor simpler. But he doesn't speak about it. As for writing about it! . . . There aren't even five pages on this subject in the whole of world literature. Everything has been analyzed, painted and repainted a thousand times, from hate to death, right up to sleep. But that moment is never mentioned. One tends to use abstract expressions such as "Supreme Voluptuousness," "Little Death." In short, one simply covers up. Well! That is because of fear.

In the orgasm (this is true of the woman as much as it is of the man) there is a mixture of violence and sweetness unequaled, it seems to me, in any other of the acts of our bodies. Perhaps the entrance into life, if we could remember it, might appear to us as tender and tearing. Perhaps the shock of death is also of the same nature. In any case, what we experience then is inextricable. We are at the height of pleasure, at the extreme point of being one with what is; we are so much ourselves that we could shout for joy; and immediately we are called back to our puny selves which we had completely forgotten, to a confusion with the universe so little personal that already we are not quite sure whether we have known pleasure.

And for the man, a rather astonishing fact should be added: he becomes someone else. For a few moments he becomes the woman. Most men cannot bear it. Nothing had prepared them for this reversal.

Consider in the course of time what a man really is: he is a gesture. One gesture only, only one act. A man is straight shoulders, a raised arm—even if that arm is sometimes a sexual member. He is an intention which does not deviate, a road between two hedges. But, for once, he is dispersed, he can no longer make a movement in a known direction, he hardly knows where he is. He has become that which spreads itself, which rushes forward, which does not yet quite exist. That which is promised, but will only be achieved with patience, that which has been received but not yet born, what lives close to him, in spite of himself, but in a future that his consciousness is unaware of. He has ceased to be what he was so proud to have been even to the exclusion of all else: a man. And this entrance into the other condition, the multiple and fluid condition, came to hit him at the moment of his greatest virility. He is stunned.

There is no retreating now. It is too late. He will have to experience this new condition until desire returns. You see that I understand my young fellow and his anger. It is surprising to what extent we are naked once we have taken you! I don't mean physiologically disarmed—which would have very little sense—but undressed, then immediately covered again with new garments, transformed, turned inside out. Maybe that is why you feel us to be falling asleep. That is not the word: absenting ourselves . . . How does one deal with fear?

95

Fear, here it comes again! I wish it were only a paradox. Alas, it isn't one. One would have to be able to see others making love, or better still to see oneself. It is a combat. The man wants to force, the woman wishes to be forced. It is a tearing. The man wants to dig, and the woman wants to be split in two. It is a competition. Arms and legs hook together; backs are squashed. It is like a kneading. And the rhythm is so often broken. The cries of enjoyment are moans. Everybody knows that, but who is amazed by it? Why are all the outer signs of love, when it is made, that is, in the moment when it has become simple, when it should be purely love, why are they all gestures of aggression? Why do couples appear to suffer so much? When will they be happy if it isn't now? I know: there are those who do not fight, but dance together. Are there many of them?

I will only speak for the man. For him, love is wild. It is always a punishment, a stroke that he inflicts. He inflicts it with more or less respect, with more or less regret; but he inflicts it. In the best of cases he wants to prove something: he will leave his mark. And I say it again; it is not malice: it is fear. Everything happens as if he were not quite sure that he can manage to make love truly, to know how to make love. As if he were never quite sure that the woman really wanted him and might at the last second chase him away. If so, he would find himself hideous, stamping with open arms in a solitary ecstasy which makes him tremble in advance. And he strikes . . . Yes, there are also couples who dance, but are there some who pray together?

There must be some, and in the future there will be more. But today, for most men, love is only an assault. Everything that is shy in them, and distant—their Self, their soul—is in a state of siege. They try to break the siege, they throw themselves forward with everything they've got, they do not look at anything—neither the women, nor themselves. They don't want to know what they are doing; they run towards the goal, which is not pleasure but deliverance. They only feel pleasure in their bodies—and even there for a very short time. Hardly have they finished when they will have to start again. Hardly have they received than they feel empty-handed, and disgust takes hold of them. They came with fear, and they leave with fear. And where is prayer in all that?

Where is it? Where is love? One should really ask oneself that question every time. After having made love, we do not think of love any longer. It is so simple! We think of its consequences, or more often than not, of ordinary life which starts again, of the life without love. Where is prayer? And if you want me to be more modest: where is the joy of being alive, the joy of having said yes, the joy of for once not having stayed inside one's own skin, stubborn and refusing, refusing everything—everything that is not ourselves? Why should one always close oneself off?

Men do not like love, I tell you. What they love is desire, and desire only; it is that which precedes love. Think of the poets, the novelists, the storytellers, of all those who have spoken about love in our name for centuries. There is always a point where they stop, and it's always the same: in front of love. They have approached it with delight. They have described the parading of the man and the detours of the woman. They have sung of the marvels every time a gesture was to be accomplished. They have undone the hair a thousand times, and unbuckled the belts. They have cried out aloud that the heart of a man when filled with desire is as strong as the whole world. They have made us believe that love, once consummated, would be the salvation of the universe. And when love is there, they become silent. I seem to have waited for years for the one who would speak of what lies beyond the waiting, beyond the dreams and the outstretched arms, beyond the excitement. And I have not found him yet.

That they all stop before the act of love, the act itself, I could understand. It is a moment when we are too deeply engaged in the very ground of our bodies to be able to run towards the light of words. But after love, why is it that they don't have voices anymore?

They do not want to say anything, they will not say anything. For them it is a time of satiation, of marriage; it is the time of habits and of the encumbrance of the flesh, the time when the faces even of those whom they've loved vanish. One would almost think that they do not wish to have anything to do with it, as with a meal that is finished. It is not worthy of words. It brings them back to an awkwardness, to all the repetitions, to this childhood in themselves which they thought they had chased away so well, to the boredom of only being what they are. Can you explain their silence in any other way?

Earlier on, during desire, they felt grand. Even if their desire had not reached its goal, they would not have ceased to believe in their grandure, because they were not singing of the victories but of the preparations. Even their wedding songs were just the preparation for a banquet! As long as the act of love has not taken place, love makes them talkative. But afterwards, they are too small. They are afraid of not having loved. Perhaps they say to themselves vaguely that there is a movement of love, the last one, which they have not been able to make. Sounds break in their throats. Images withdraw from their eyes. There is a man who has become forgetfulness, a woman who has become substance. How could one express this?

One would be able to do so if one had lived it properly. A human couple—in spite of the poets, it is after love that one can assess it. It is those moments which provide the right measure, and not the exalted searching which precedes it. It is then, and then only that there is a balance between matter and desire. It is then that our shells open a little—never earlier—and that we become quietly a little bit more than a man, a little bit more than a woman. If there is a sacred place in love, that is the one. One has to say so at all costs. Otherwise, the body of the woman becomes this thick, sliding rock. It is a wall. It is another rock of Sisyphus . . .

So I'm going to say it! . . . I am willing to try, but with you. I don't mind, on condition that later on, one day, you show the same courage, and that you speak of love after love as it exists for a woman. Because it seems to me that it should rather be the woman who begins. It seems to me that they know more about it than we do. And it doesn't matter anyway! But there is yet another condition: that you stop me each time that I am not sufficiently precise. These subjects are in the last resort so obscure, and they are poorly made for words. You promise that you will stop me?

After love. This is what I mean by it: it is when the body of the man and the woman are not yet separate. It is that moment and no other. Because even in resting side by side, something else has already started. It is during those brief minutes when their bodies cannot be distinguished. So, for instance, this experience after love could not exist when men applied, and most of them did, the old method of contraception, "coitus interruptus." And that is why to my mind it was a bad practice.

So they are together and they can hardly know who is the woman and who is the man, because the man doesn't attack anymore, can no longer attack. That, is the great event. Before the orgasm the man was imposing himself. Even if he was called and received, his presence was that of a stranger. He was an instrument that opens and breaks. In the moments of greatest abandon he was still a force that passes. And that was his honor: that is how he knew himself to be a man. Neither he nor the woman would have wanted to renounce it. For both of them there was a rejoicing: the fact of being two, one who hollows out and the other who hollows herself. A great rejoicing, because there is a unique happiness to feel at this point so different. It is as if one were suddenly to see oneself strongly confirmed in one's being when a kind of laughter takes hold of you, a wish to shout: "I'm here!" However, as long as the man is working upon the woman, it is separation. One has to know that. It is a void, a vertigo, the sensation of which renders them mad with pleasure. But the pleasure is always mixed with rage. Even the tenderest of the acts of love is still a rape.

The man attacks. It is his way of giving. The woman knows it and always hopes that he will attack a little more. He gives what he has, and that is really a refusal. Ah! If women in the act of love would only look at the face of their men more often, they would see this refusal! Even under the most favorable circumstances, for instance, when the man and the woman both long to have a child, there is on the part of the man a contraction and a retreat. There is that panic to be so strongly what he is, but that it lasts so little time. There is that conviction that during those few instants it will no longer be up to him to play a part, but for her, and I mean nature, in other words, this unknown in which he does not participate. As long as life is a current that flows through him and makes a drawn bow of his sexual organ, the man wishes to be and thinks of himself as generous: he gives his arrows. But that is all that he gives. And when suddenly he no longer has this power to wound, then it is either escape—in sleep or in anger—or it is finally love. Love for the first time.

To find oneself in the depth of the being that one loves and not to be able to change anything anymore. To have given everything one had to give and to add what the will has as its most precious element, no longer to want. Isn't it a priceless experience? And this seed that came forth from you, which is much more rich and living than all the fortune you had invested in desire, which is more real than you,—and which, however, had chosen you to be born—this seed is now in her body at a point where you can't distinguish it. Both pleasures and all the fluids that have arisen from both bodies are simply one. It is then that we have to rejoice for a second time, but more ardently than before. It is then that we must remember who it is that we love, because to the love making in which we were engaged a moment ago with all its violence, another love has been added: that which happens in spite of ourselves.

"In spite of ourselves" "to want no longer," that is not **our** language, you are right: it is yours. Men refuse to abandon themselves. It is their greatness. But in love, it is their stupidity. You are so much more in tune. You are so, at the point of not claiming your turn to possess. Nevertheless, when the sexual organ of the man has rested in yours, when he has recovered his sweetness and his childhood state, it is no longer he who possesses you—it is you, it is really you who possesses him. And now you see, the roles are reversed; the man must consent. He must do so, not only because it is true and if we wish love to be complete we must only tolerate in it that which is real, we must chase away all belief; but moreover, because there is in this inversion of the functions, the brightest promise which can be made to a couple, the brightest and perhaps the only one which does not imply any conditions.

If a man were always a man from the beginning to the end of lovemaking and if he were only that, and if the woman would remain woman eternally, there would be no love. Quite simply, there wouldn't be any. Instead there would be this irritable, impoverished substitute: desire. There would be this endless, renewed tension. There would only be greedy, blind individuals who throw themselves continually on one another, who hurt one another, who hurry and trample each other, who finally don't want to love one another. But the time after love has been given to us.

I have become a man. I have just become one inasmuch as nature allows it. I have been the mover, and the one who made way; and also the one who doesn't take that into consideration. I have been active to the point of insolence, to the point of turning away all dreams. This fever—because it is one—could have gripped me for the rest of my life. What would I have learned then? I would only have known myself. But quite suddenly, my body who knows better than I what is needed, changes directions: I have got to go towards the other extreme of nature, towards you. For a while, my body gives me the condition of a woman, the condition I wanted the least, the condition where I have my only chance of discovering you. And it is your turn now to take and to master. You will finally be able to know me.

After having made love, everything would be so joyful if the man could remember that at best he is only half a being, and if the woman also had that same memory! It is in the alternating of the sexes that love consists. One day it will be in their reunion. But if their reuniting is meant for a future which we do not yet perceive, the alternation is here: we only have to live it. Experiencing it, even only after each embrace, we are happy, we will be happy. Yet it is more than that: we are released. This burning lead that was desire, suddenly vanishes. This weight in our bones, right in our eyelids, and in our throats, which we call flesh, is suddenly lifted up. Remember! After love, we know so well that lightening. It is a real transparency. It is as if the movements of love released smoke from our bodies. It is as if the sexual act, because of its being matter, had extracted us from matter. It is the beginning of another condition.

Now this lightening, what has it to do with pleasure? Almost nothing, it's true. And also one has to say: it comes from somewhere else. Well! Without this pleasure, if it hadn't been considerable on both our parts, we would not have known this lightening. Nevertheless, it is a lightness of a kind that is totally new: it is not a satisfaction. It is . . . but I'm not quite ready to say it. Let me first talk to you about pleasure.

It brings as much pain as it does joy. I'm surprised that we mention it so little. Pleasure in love is a caress, or a bite; nobody knows. It has waves that burn, some pinch. Something is about to break. Love has moments that are too weak and that exasperate one. It has others that are so sharp that one would like to get rid of them. It pierces you in the back like a fork, or it gets bored. And above all, the way it comes to an end! For the man, it stops at the instant when it is about to become immense, when it was no longer going to crawl, but to stand up and lift you with it. It is brief like a catastrophe. It has no substance.

As soon as we speak of love, everything is falsified because we speak in terms of need. The needs of the body, appetite, the raging hunger and its satisfaction. Ecstasy itself, we pretend that it is nothing other than pleasure, beginning with it and finishing with it. Why don't we tell the truth? Pleasure is but one moment of love. It is the dangerous moment, dangerous because it is ambiguous; it marks that turning point where we haven't given anything yet and we haven't received anything either. It accompanies us towards love, at the most. But this strange companion, we will have to let go of him.

We shall have to, if we want to experience joy (I said earlier, lightening), if we want to love. For as long as we are involved in pleasure, we are simply stubborn, we do not love. We are bumping around, each one for himself, against the power, against expansion. We are forces in a cage. It is after making love that love really begins.

We need not search any longer. Isn't that a joy without comparison? Bad work has come to an end! You are not the one that I take and, God be praised, you are no longer the one I have. I have nothing, you have nothing. We have emerged from what our bodies wanted on their own, from what they did or didn't know how to do. We have become smooth like a hand (you see, even in me there is nothing that resists any longer). We are no longer owners. It isn't up to us to be rich any longer. It isn't up to us to renew the assets. It's up to life to pass over us: it fashions us, it uses the hollow space. You are no longer yourself, and you are no longer an obstacle. And I don't ask for anything. We are together.

Has the desire gone? Surely we are not going to shed any tears over it! It has left our bodies, but I'm sure you feel it: it's all around us, it carries us. It has gone back where it came from. It still stretches your body. And it makes mine into something other than a machine. Yes indeed, it is desire, but such as it is when we do not force it. You see, desire enlightens us.

How one could wish that all men and all women would experience with eyes wide open this departure—or rather this flight—of desire! Because desire is an element, like air and fire (and almost everyone ignores that), an element which existed before we took hold of it, and when we loosen our hand it is still there. Let's not be ridiculous: it doesn't belong to us. With open eyes, everyone would see that it still touches them. They would feel its hand on them which softens and takes out the wrinkles, takes hold of their two bodies and allows them, finally, because they are no longer intervening, to penetrate one another. But with what fingers it takes hold of them! No clumsy heaviness any longer, no emptiness to be filled, no tearing, no trace of vengeance. Isn't that lightness?

If there is a moment in love when one would want to cry out, "stop! you are so beautiful!," **that** is the one. It is the time when seeds are sown. And I'm not specifically thinking of the child (although that possibility, perhaps a distant one, makes the soul and the body tremble, and sometimes brings them together to the point of ecstasy), but I'm thinking of the couple. The couple is becoming established in the moments that follow love. Do people know about this?

They think that everything depends on the attitude they had before making love. It is to this stage that they apply all their rules of morality and their taboos. For them, there are good ways of making love and bad ones. There are all the imperatives of respect, delicacy, the interminable waiting, the half-formed gestures, indirect words, considerations of time and place, the feelings one proclaims instead of desire. The one who doesn't play the game is, for them, a brute. Haven't you noticed it? Sexual morality refers particularly to the pre-liminaries. Morality no longer holds good once we are engaged in the act. And after love all scruples can go to the devil. Idiots. That is just the time that one must have respect!

Fantasy takes hold of me (more often than you can believe) to say to men: "Desire your women as you wish, desire them brutally if that turns you on, if that is the tone on which you like them. Treat them in your desire as goddesses or as harlots. What does it change? You are not going to do anything different to them after your hypocrisies than you would do without them. It is not now that you have to take hold of yourself. And in any case, they are not keen on your cautious ways. And it's not during love either. But it's after . . .

Afterwards, everything is a serious matter. Love is in suspense. It is a bit like a bad dream. The slightest thought which might be strange to it can hurt even beyond reversal. The harm that we do when, after love, instead of thinking about love we think of our houses, our worries, our checks! What a massacre if, at this moment, we do not adore this woman (whoever she is, even if she happens to be a prostitute), who has allowed herself to be inhabited, right to her very blood! There is not a single vile act, however gross it may be, that we have committed before making love which can hurt so much.

I said that one had to adore. And in fact, it is a duty. It is in fact, in the course of time, the first of all the duties that love imposes upon us. Early on it seemed that none existed. But what is essential is to love love. Because the desire is there, but it has changed its sign: it is no longer personal. This scandal, that earlier on we could only love for ourselves and for ourselves alone, has been erased. They and we (and it is high time), we are finally in love with the same desire. And the illusion that it has disappeared, that is the misery of the couples; it is not their truth.

Will we ever know how this madness was disseminated which makes of desire only a passing and frivolous state, and which makes us believe that once satisfied, it dies? Women are less subject to this myth than we are. And yet it seems at times that we have converted them. Desire has many faces. It is in absences, it is in caresses, it is in the lovemaking itself. Each time it is a different degree of itself. But in the love that has been made, desire is more completely there than anywhere else. Then it hovers over the couple. It is no longer a shock, no longer a trembling, it no longer plants itself on a point in their bodies, making them dance like marionettes without a master. It becomes a breathing through their limbs. It touches the eyes as well as it does the sexual organs. It flows from the flesh to something other than the flesh. It promises new states of life.

It is quite true! I said "towards something other than the flesh": I mean new states, a new condition. I have not been tender toward pleasure. It is not that I am uncomfortable with the body. I will even tell you this: I belong to those (and there are not so many of them), who love the bodies of men and of women, who always love them when they are being used for love. I know that they are not all that wise, and that they transport with them a whole heritage of possession and of poverty. I see how they repeat themselves and do not progress. I know their terrible jealousy. But I love them, those bodies: they are the earth and we are on earth.

When I feel like leaping into the heavens, it is with them. No, the body does not bother me. I understand that there are people who wish to get around it. I have even sometimes admired the love that comes about without it. But these types of love are not my business. I want to carry everything upward, everything that has been given to us. And the body has been given to us; I'm not about to forget it.

Also, when I speak of new states, I'm thinking in another way: I think of the crossing. If I make love, immediately it is a current that I experience, the passage of a current. From the first minute onwards, and even before any gesture has taken place, a force takes hold of me. It takes hold of my roots. I become circulation; my whole body is agitated. But soon it is no longer alone: another body is working with it. And it happens within them. I like to feel it; I would like to feel it to a greater extent; I am only chagrined if I don't feel it sufficiently. But it also happens in spite of them. We act so little in making love. We are like containers.

We are lamps that are lit, vases that are filled. Not even that: we are a place crossed by will. And to wish to persuade us, as many will want to do, that this will is ours, has always seemed insignificant to me. It is so clear that it is simply not that. This will comes from far away. It works so powerfully in us , both on what is and what is not our body, that finally it envelopes all of our deeds, reducing them to simple rites of obedience.

Let's obey, that's good. The will works so powerfully that it doesn't stop at the physical. Procreation cannot be the end of love; it can only be an episode. The episode was so agreeable that most human beings stop short at this point. But there is a continuation. And I am crazy about what happens next.

As far as pleasure is concerned, I have simply said that it is poorly experienced. Because in order to be able to forget it, to enter into that lightness which is so much superior, I know too well that one must have known it. I have nothing against pleasure, but against its weakness. Ah! If pleasure were only as great as we dream it to be. I only have something against our weakness which prevents us from experiencing it to the very end, which constantly retards the moment when we would be able to transform it. A couple that has never experienced climax will never know what desire is. Be sure of that. The sunny side of desire, the one where personal conditions have disappeared, where there is no longer this "I want you and you resist me," this condition where peace installs itself and promises to remain, the couple will never know that.

Love is a crossing. Anything that stops it is a fault and there are twenty ways of stopping it. All it takes is to forbid it within oneself. Sometimes it's called purity. But from which impurity is one protecting oneself? All it takes is, to make love the way we eat—and the meal finished, there is nothing left to eat. All it takes is, when love is hardly finished, to leave slamming the door. Each time it is a desertion. Love is a crossing, a journey. We are so made that all the flowers and all the pebbles on the road can enter our skins. We are so made that we can be loved when we ourselves love. And it is not the woman who loves the man, or the man who loves the woman, not solely that: they are loved together.

You see that everything is in its right place: the body and the soul. You see that love enters our bodies, becomes flesh, turns out to be heavier than ourselves—the heaviest and most tenacious part of ourselves—but also that it escapes. After having made love our bodies are there, but we look at them. That is even the only moment given to us when we can look at them. And if they have been good roads, if they allowed love to travel well, they are beautiful, they are simple. They have never been so simple.

7

And supposing we had liberated it too early? Imagine the consequences. And if we had rushed through in fifty years what should have taken us centuries; if we had forgotten that love, of all the human powers, is the least advanced (less ready, oh yes! much less ready than intelligence itself); if we had lost the very memory of how love blinds, known so well in the past, which makes it hesitate perpetually between rape and sacrifice; if we no longer knew that between the two it can only do one thing: obey the laws of its time; if we had to guard ourselves from treating it like a man, he who is only a child! . . . could we still save it?

I know that I will not prove anything. My fears are not in fashion. I know that it is no longer possible to deal with love as one did a hundred years ago. I know that it could not be hidden any longer because that game is repulsive. I know too that we have to look at it differently, simply to look at it. I prefer the ways of today. I accept more willingly our risks than the lies of the past. But love is in danger. I see clearly that it is in danger.

Am I contradicting myself? If that is the case, I don't worry much about it. Love must be right, not I. What would we become if it were being lost?

I will not prove anything, but I need to reiterate that: love is in danger. Today because it is talked about in the newspapers and advertised on the walls, millions of people believe that they know where it is. They believe that it is no longer a menace. From one day to the next they are going to forget that it is a promise. Indifference has begun. Look at young people. You don't see it on their faces? I hear it in their voices. There are so many who don't even realize any longer that their destiny hangs on the thread of love, depends on the image that they make of it, like a single thread which cannot be bought in our society of abundance. They no longer see that between copulation and charity there is an unexplored region—virgin, yes, almost virgin—fragile, untreatable matter with which men have always played, yet fundamentally neglected. Matter? If you prefer, I'll call it a current, a passage. What I'm afraid of is that the current will be cut . . . We will have to count on instinct: it recharges the batteries. But what I'm afraid of, is that the instinct too will disappear. No fact will prove it, no statistic. Be assured: I am not going to look for that type of proof. What I am afraid of, is that we are in the process of killing love with facts.

But not long ago, it was with judgements that one killed it. Was that preferable? It had been decided that love was matter, the most sly form of matter, one that can best attack the spirit, and if it were given free rein it would consume the spirit; so love was domesticated. By means of laws—laws of the church, laws of society—it was chased away from the only realm where human beings can experience it: the meeting between their souls and their bodies. Bawdiness was tolerated because it was only the body that was involved. It was more difficult to bear feelings—but one bore them anyway—because in those feelings the soul is reduced to a degree which is least compromising of all: that of the heart. They were running, if you will, from the *Decameron* to *The New Heloise*, from the fantasies of the flesh to those of the imagination. The trick was well played, there was no love.

There was some, nevertheless. Yes, but forbidden; I mean regulated. Regulated for the use of all, for the human masses. Placed under high surveillance in such a way that here and there accidents came about, but never freedom. Reduced to extremes: to the act of the flesh or to the abnegation of the flesh. Hidden on the pretext of prudishness, security, salvation. Divested of its center, which can only be an exchange.

The technique was simple: allowing people to open their eyes on love without love, since no one could have prevented them anyway. Authorizing debauchery; regretting it, but allowing it. Or otherwise allowing people to open their eyes on love beyond love, where, so to speak, it isn't up to them to play anymore. And for the rest, throwing a veil of silence over what happens between them when they love.

"One must not look at love." Hasn't that been the invisible decree of our societies for centuries? One was not supposed to look at love, each time that it belonged to human beings and only to them, each time when it was the concern of two people who perhaps would not find very much, or who might not find anything at all, but who were ready to seek everything through love. Not to look at it was a stricter order, it seems to me, than not to show it. For in the last resort, reduced to debauchery, love is not beautiful and one needn't fear that it will seduce. But to arrange things in such a way that couples would always unite in the night; that was the basic idea. To instruct them never to know fully the gestures which they make, and surely not to name them. And if, nevertheless, they were about to discover words, true ones, to substitute meaningless replacements as soon as possible: words of feeling. To throw couples into the vagueness of instincts. And sexual desire helped the whole thing along, because it is in any case that which in us is least clear and doesn't desire any clarity at all. To force couples to forget that they are two, when they make love, and that they start the whole adventure again. To persuade them from mother to daughter and from one silence to the next that love does not belong to them, and that it is society who lends it to them, that it is a theft, always a theft, or at least petty pilfering. And if the couples in love were sufficiently distracted, if they closed their eyes as soon as the first caresses began, if they no longer felt that they were embarking on a unique journey but on the journey which everybody makes—the same always the same—then love would no longer be a danger.

We have other needs, and couldn't do it any longer. Yet does that make our task easier? There is a freedom that we have lost, and that they all had in the past. When this movement began in them, for which they hardly had a name, (and which we today call sexuality and about which we reason—but do we really know it any better?), this movement so obscure and essential was, it's obvious, invented outside of ourselves, they didn't have to ask themselves what it was. They simply had to bear it. A freedom. That is too stiff a word. But at least a consolation. It must have been a consolation to feel oneself taken in the moment of love, when one no longer knows why one is doing so well what one is doing, why what one is doing is fatal to such an extent, when a hand which is not yours directs your gestures and knows what is going to happen. How many women in particular must have for centuries felt strangled with sweetness, as they felt themselves giving themselves without mercy! And not only to the man who had been chosen for them, but to the world from which the man came, to the earth, to the land into which they were plunging; to the past of their race, its laws, its future; to all those forces that had made women of them and had been fixed outside of them and which they never questioned! To be a part of generations, no longer to know during the instant that you love, if you love, or if it is your mother or the mother of your mother, or one day your daughter. To enter into the flow, to feel yourself impregnated by everything that you do not know, everything that has been decided by society, by life, but never by yourself . . . To feel that life is another name for death. Because every woman, and that wasn't so long ago, could have died in childbirth. She could have, and she knew it. And her child might die at an early age; and she was resigned to it. Giving herself both to life and to death; to know that the choice is not yours . . . There were then other dreams. And if today we no longer love those dreams, let's not believe that millions in the past did not love them.

I repeat it: our happiness, our new happiness, is to have discovered that the love that we make is ours, that nobody, not even from a distance, has the right to tell us what it means and what it is for, that all its laws are usurpations, that it is not an unmixed happiness. Now we must look at love and really read it (and it's no easier reading than in the past) to count its movements, to ask ourselves if they are the best ones they could be, to find ourselves again in our insufficiency, to persuade ourselves that it suffices. And after that, is it surprising that love has become today the home of all solitude?

Just recall this for a moment. The lovers of the past were never alone; they never said they were. Even Tristan and Isolde, for them to believe that they were alone for a moment, they needed a potion! Their bodies were there, separated in the usual way, but they were going to roll into the universal body. One is never alone with one's people; and one is surely not alone with one's sin. Your sin wouldn't leave you. Heloise and Abelard were never alone.

But today love is emptiness. It is every time the threat of emptiness. It is this enormous adventure of breaking the solitude and meeting one knows not what. It is exploration; it is no longer obedience. And it is certainly not a greater happiness. Has anyone ever seen happiness put up with such a mass of doubt?

Happiness or not, that has come to an end for the time being: people are not going to go back to obedience, not as it was in the past. Psychoanalysis has come over them. Now we photograph love, we teach it. Eroticism is being sold. Tomorrow pornography will receive its official stamp of approval. Love is no longer a secret. We give it a face and we deface it. Am I happy?

I should be, I, who was telling you the other day that love should not simply be an instinct anymore. I should howl with the wolves: "The sexual revolution has begun. Long live the revolution!" I've always experienced shame and silence about love as faults. I saw, and still see them as a delay. The Self has to be liberated. If it isn't free during love it will not be anywhere else, not even in politics. I was waiting for this freedom. There it is, and I might not wish it any longer!

But everybody announces it, and nobody holds it. Love was a discovery; it was not a spectacle. We are only given the spectacle. When I say, "to look at love," by that I mean, "with my eyes." It is "the Love that I make." Love, like life, can't be caught from a distance. If there is one thing in the world which is not objective and which can't be, must not be, would die if it ever became objective, that indeed is love. The couple that copulates in London on the stage, all those "biology lessons" that one hears of in Denmark, are not even scandalous. What do you imagine that they can teach us? They are simply objects.

I was asking for a beholding, and what they give me is a spectacle. And they want me to be satisfied! But the most useless thing is always the spectacle; it's the belief that whatever it is can happen without us; it is this lie: love is there, it's all ready-made, you just have to take it, see how it functions, you simply have to imitate it, see! It wasn't even terrible; it is this plot: love is an object. Whether you take it from above or from below, whether you feel like it or whether you are blasé, it's always the same. Just go around it and it will no longer frighten you. It is when it frightens you that you figure out that it is yours—we call that your complexes. It is this sickness: showing everything and expecting nothing from those to whom one shows it. Oh, that's a modern one! But there is another: wishing to require that there be only one love, a single love-object, the same for all in the same circumstances, the same at the same age, the same at the same level of culture. No! What is only a spectacle is not my business. It should be the concern of no one. It is a noise, one more, in a world where there is no more voice. Why would I want it? But as for really looking . . . and really looking at love is the most uncertain of enterprises (oh how good that it should be so!), it is also the most necessary. I believe it to be urgent. That is what I am thinking about.

There is no intimacy in love. Does intimacy equal being in love? We have simply invented the word in order to hide the fact. The fact has to be brought out into the clear daylight again: what we do in this intimacy of which we are so jealous, what we do behind our closed doors and our curtains and our murmurings, in our darkened rooms, under the clothes which cover us, that doesn't belong to us. This sense of modesty itself, it would seem that we were only keen about it in order to protect us from the eyes of others, but it reveals something about us. A couple that loves belongs to society. It can't escape from it. It doesn't escape in marriage because it is society itself which gave marriage to the couple. Society knows where a couple stands, measures its gestures, compounds and claims the results in advance, keeps an eye on the couple. But no more so if the relationship is illicit, for then the couple must lie, and that lie, society has known it through the ages, pursues it, denounces it and makes of it a property as publicly as marriage itself. And however much lovers think that for once they might be able to realize the impossible secret, society sticks to their heels: it is in their habits. Every act of love is ancestral: it began a thousand years ago, and we never bring it to an end. It goes so far that this dream, of dealing with one woman and with one man in particular, with a being that one could not possibly confuse with another, a being who would appear only once and that we alone would have known, this dream of perfect loving intimacy is never realized. Behind this woman that you wish to be unique in the world, there is a mother, and all the sisters you have or could have had, and all the children that she will give you, would give you if you allow her to. And you, for her, you are no longer her lover but her father, or her son already; you represent all those who one day became the masters of all the women who preceded her, and to whom she is related by blood. You are the one she loves, but she doesn't think of you alone just as little as you think only of her; you are the violence and the law and the tenderness of the law. There is no two-person solitude.

And then there is the body which is the same for all. There is this perpetual scandal of all bodies looking alike: one woman slides into the memory of another and prepares for new ones to come. Differences, yes, there certainly are some. But when they come from the body, and from its forms, are we really quite sure that we owe those differences to the body? Isn't it rather to our feelings? There is this discord between the soul which wishes to be mine and which wishes to meet yours—no other—and the body which is like a continuous piece of cloth that unrolls itself and cradles in its folds all the women who have ever been, who are, and who will be. The souls separate and the bodies mix. Nevertheless, to make the soul pass through the body, to implant what belongs only to ourselves into that which belongs only to the universe, love cannot be anything but that. Wasn't I right to call it an adventure? Not something expected, not a function: an adventure.

And in which, if one of the parts is mistreated, then everything falls apart. An adventure, the outcome of which depends on the slightest forgetfulness; so fragile a circulation that it is always about to be sidetracked, perverted. Love is of this world, and yet isn't. And if the body is treated as better than the soul, or the soul as better than the body, it will no longer grow.

After all, our century is perhaps not all that bad: it concerns itself with the body, admits its needs, seeks to educate it, brings it back into the daylight, shows it, displays it. I don't know whether it goes too far. Complete nudity was perhaps not necessary to that extent. But there was so much that we had to take back. We had been wrapped in such a silence, so much hypocrisy which did so much harm! Because if we deny the body and wrap it up in veils and caution, it is then that it will seek revenge. It likes to avenge itself. Forbid a man or a woman to think of the body, make them take up the habit of bracketing it as soon as they make use of it, make them believe that when they look at it or name it they commit a fault against integrity or some other respectability, and immediately the misery begins, and the desire to share the misery with others.

To share it, yes! But more often than not to give it. There have been dark moments for love, and they were not so long ago. Man used woman as an opportunity to ignore what he was. He approached her like an unstable object, irritating, inferior. Why should he have bothered to learn what this object was made of? It was not himself and that was sufficient. It was different from him to the point of condescension. Power for one and docility for the other. And so the love of bodies was a mere accident, a type of embarrassment, an episode that one conceals under the blanket of marriage or of passion and of which, above all, one never speaks. It was high time for our century to exaggerate.

If it goes too far, at least it is going. The man is about to find his body again, and the woman hers, and an opportunity arises for both of them: to renounce cruelty. To approach a woman like someone unknown and to have, before anything else, to tear her beneath her veils; that incites one to do damage. To receive a man whom one has forbidden oneself to look at, that makes one feel like despising and pretending. Who could regret that we have placed the body under the bright light of day? I simply believe that we are stopping along the way.

Possibly we may have taken a wrong road. To show the body doesn't mean to know much about it. To see it everywhere is not to really look at it. I don't mind the exhibition:

it is more ridiculous than harmful; but I do fear the illusions into which it throws us. On the pretext that today we are saying everything in books and letting everything pass on our screens, we are ready to believe that the matter is settled: love no longer has shadows, love belongs to everybody, love is the first of all the collective goods . . . Collective, no doubt, but on condition that it is reclaimed each time for the secret account of each individual. And who says this today?

My male body, is not essentially different from the bodies of all men. The body of a woman is the body of a woman. We had to be reminded of it. But once this humility has been discovered again, and which was in fact necessary, I say: "that's enough!" Love has not been made for the community. And to look at it, doesn't mean looking at others doing it, but to look at oneself doing it.

And there, everything has to be re-invented. To begin, we have to unlearn, because we have been taught not to see love. We have made of it an interruption of dignity: desire must be assumed; let it be assumed without us! To look at oneself in love, or even to turn one's eyes to the other when sex brings us back to bestiality! And in any case, what is there to see? The anatomy is the same for all, and the combinations are piddling. Fantasy—fantasy itself is here devoid of imagination. Were the movements of lovemaking for Antony and Cleopatra not the same as for that little couple living on the sixth floor? Someone should cover those things as quickly as possible! Love is neither made for the spirit nor for the eyes: it is a matter of experiencing it. It belongs to the darkness. It came about out of its own without our having asked for it, may it run away on its own! . . .

So the first step is to unlearn. We need to forget the way people have told us about it. To get out of this alternative, where love is in prison: either the feelings (for them the word "caress" is the last one, beyond which ugliness begins) or the physiology (and here the word "coitus" says everything). We should know that the true words, which really express what we see, do not exist. And how could they possibly exist when nine times out of ten we throw ourselves into lovemaking as we do into a hole with red and black shadows? Everything needs to be re-invented.

You must admit it is a strange abdication: people who normally inquire into everything, who try to read into the faces, and into the lines of the hand, who pay attention to the slightest gestures, mimicry, and behavior and who are persuaded that the expression around the mouth, the way we walk, right down to our clothes, reveal who we are—as soon as it comes to love, they want no longer to read. Could it be that for them the parts of our body which are involved are too lowly? That is certainly how they've been considered for centuries. Is that still where we are? They are so close, so miserably close to the organs of excretion, they have been placed in such a bizarre way by Nature, they seem so material that it is repugnant to endow them with spirit . . . But who is not aware that they are only material because of the extent of our disdain and nothing else? Everything has to be unlearnt, everything has to be displaced.

If we look at love, it's true that if we see it as the intertwining of two fleshly bodies, we simply become bored; if we see it as the gradual approach of two desires, the one towards the other, usually confused and unequal, that is inevitable, we become rather disgusted. But to look—for me, that is radically different: it is to witness a return. The sexual organ of a man resembles so little the one of a woman and yet they are the same, inverted. The organ of a man is so cruelly isolated from that of the woman; and yet this permission which is not given during the other hours of life, in making love suddenly it touches our bodies, orders the forms of our bodies, and makes everything in them respond to each other: it is union. "Union," the word hides the wonder: it is a new sexual organ which is born, a complete one. And it is one that we should not be content simply to experience, but that should be seen.

The dimensions and the beauty of it should be inquired into as one reads a face: detail by detail. It is that for which our languages do not have any words.

It's not enough to accept the body in love. It's certainly wiser and more generous than to refuse it, and I admit that during the last fifty years we have made some progress in this respect. But we have to make the leap, and know it after having accepted it.

There is a saying which maintains that a man who can love rightly does not think of himself in the process. That is silly! If the man forgets about his sexual organ for one single moment, loses sight of it so to speak, and doesn't place himself like a plant in its sap, he will never know the sexual organ of the woman. And the woman is under the same law. The rise of pleasure, each one must experience the stages of it, one by one, mercilessly. It is only then that this other sex, the one towards which they both run individually, will have a chance of bursting forth. And, when it will be there, all this jumble of organs, this isolation and this dispersion that they have experienced as a temptation, but also a shame, this thickness which was taking away their taste for seeing, all that will have disappeared. Nevertheless, there is one condition: that is that nothing during the whole process of making love has been held back or hidden; that no vibration of the body has passed for inconsequent, that they have kept, both of them from beginning to end, their eyes open, and they have respected everything. Shall I tell you what I think? The couple capable of listening to the least movement of these two bodies, lent to the couple for love, this couple would break the chain and the souls would enter . . . The souls that usually are excluded from love and who hold their vigil from afar, not properly engaged, would finally feel called and received. They would set themselves to work. But the condition is this yes given to the body, this all-inclusive yes.

It is at least one of the terms of the contract, and I don't mean the contract between a particular man and a particular woman (that particular contract doesn't really concern me, because even if it thinks of itself as eternal, I know very well that it isn't) but for all human beings on the earth there is a contract between their condition of being human and the rest of creation; there is an equilibrium, of which the clauses are stern. One of them is that nothing will be experienced in the soul which has not been lived through to begin with in the body. And a corollary: nothing will be accomplished in the body which has not been achieved in the soul at the same instant. This is a contract of love; one has to honor it, otherwise love goes away.

Look at them, the human beings. From century to century, they run from one excess of the soul to an excess of the body, and consequently from one infidelity to another. Either they do not want to hear about the body or they dismiss the soul. It is always Petrarch or "Hair." And I admit that at present, the soul is not enjoying its greatest days. Nevertheless, without the marriage of the two (and how much I would like to reserve this great word, "marriage," for that union!) there is no longer love, there isn't even pleasure. Pleasure still hangs around for a moment in that area. It has its own force of inertia like everything that moves. But it slows down, and it will take its leave. Don't you see that the number of couples who make love without hope is on the increase?

The soul, always the soul! I haven't got another word for it. Let us say that for us there is a home, the body, but it has to be inhabited. One of those crazy findings of our times is that one has to inhabit every room. But "home" doesn't convey the fact well: it is a place of passage. And there is no better circumstance in life to learn about it than in love. Love is a path one enters, it is a country which one traverses, it is a road at the end of which one wishes at all costs to know what there is, it is a corridor from which one seeks the exit. And what is so astonishing, is that this is true right into its physical forms. But there is also the traveler: that is the soul; and I am going to continue calling it that.

The soul was there before the process of lovemaking began. It will be there afterwards. It only crosses through the body in love in order to make us forget the body. But wait! It would not exist quite—and surely we wouldn't be able to feel it—if it didn't take the body as a road—if it didn't count the milestones one by one. It is not the aim of the soul to reject the body. When I say that it will make us forget the body, it is because the soul will transform it. It won't stop until the body is all transformed. For the soul, the body is not a trap (it is only a trap if the body has broken off with the soul): it is a dough. The soul takes it in her hands. The soul needs the body in order to create forms or to destroy forms, to change us.

And then it is distance. Even engaged to the point of passion there is always something in the soul which distances itself. Only the body believes that it is self- sufficient; that is its way of using itself up and disappearing. The soul is a perpetual expectation of what is to come. That is what makes us, when our bodies unite, throw ourselves beyond them, to lose the taste of their limitations. That is what makes us start again. Because one doesn't make love just once; one tries and tries again and it is not because one is attracted only by pleasure.

The soul, that is what makes a drama of love because it meets the body and wants to go beyond. Either it's war, when the body resists; or it is an exploration. Never a *fait accompli*, never a possession; never an acknowledgement that could just as well be replaced by another one. Never an institution.

But what could possibly have got hold of me that I would wish to describe to you what the soul is? This is actually the first time that this has happened to me. In fact, the real question that I am asking myself is: who uses the soul today? Who makes it come into love? Today, I am afraid, fewer and fewer people. I was speaking of progress, of discoveries; but they were all on the side of the body.

To invite the soul into love, to give it a small space, wasn't it easier in the past? It was easier when love was an instinct, it was hardly a matter of the individual, but of the race. There was maternity, this imperative condition that the child should come, and this was not contested by anybody. There was this omnipresence of the future in all the gestures of lovemaking, this appetite for the future, this necessity that humanity should continue, this incessant battle against its death, this benediction when each time a child survived. There was, when men and women united, this law of welding themselves to something other than themselves and of almost forgetting themselves.

I know: that soul to which they abandoned themselves then, was not really their own. It was that of their nation, of their race; it was that of the species—and very often only that. Nevertheless it hooked into their personal soul, sometimes awakened it and taught it respect. And respect is as valuable as knowledge. Sometimes it is worth more than partial knowledge. It is today that the soul is difficult—at least in our countries—because it is ours and it is not really ours. All our destinies have become personal. Who today would still make love for his country?

Love is difficult. Love is leaving. So now we have to learn how to use the soul in it. It is now that we must interweave it into every gesture that we make and allow the soul to transform them one by one. And if there is one gesture where we have not received it, something is lying in wait for us, which is worse than shame: lethargy, perhaps one day hate. Because if we no longer love each other each time to make children, if we no longer make them except at our own hour, and if we give ourselves the right to emerge from the stream of births, if we wish no longer to be the instruments of love, and pretend to become its guardians, then sexuality must change completely. It must then have another task. It must then teach us what we cannot learn by instinct. It must become another humanity within humanity. Is that possible? It will only come about if we begin.

At the time when men and women did not love one another for themselves except on rare holiday occasions, a certain harshness was allowed. To penetrate into a woman, for instance, was for a man like a break-in, but necessary. If the work is to be done in the house, one would have to enter the house. It was just a moment of work, and the man had no reason to separate it from other such tasks. All the other tasks would follow. Today we do not have the same rights.

It is not that our deeds have changed. But if we expect other consequences from our deeds, we no longer have the same rights towards them, and we have other duties. We have to know—yes, even that—that the moment of penetration is a strange one, a unique moment; the moment when our bodies, which so many laws condemned to live in isolation (it's worse than that; outside one another) for once that is where they would meet. They do more: each one begins to feel the other, and feels the other from where it is taking place: from within. And it is a shock, if the soul is there to see it, and there has been no similar example in the rest of our lives. Up to now the kiss, only the kiss, could have prepared us for it; but that was only a mirror image. Suddenly the man is inside the woman: he doesn't see her any longer; he lives her. He lives something which is no longer simply himself. And for the woman, the man is no longer this absolute stranger, this block placed in the world, in front of her. From now onwards, each one lives not only his or her own sensations, but also those of the other. If they think this impossible, it is because they haven't paid attention, they have been carried away, and they haven't learnt yet to make love in the light.

Do you feel the whole difference? And to what extent today crudity cannot be allowed any longer?

If it's a question of the movements of lovemaking—those of the man inside the woman and those of the woman meeting him—then it is even more serious. Because if these movements are reduced to the body, made for the growth and fulfillment of pleasure and nothing else, it is hardly possible to think about them. They are in a blind race, they look like an escape, they are already finished and we haven't seen them. In any case, did we really wish to see them? But if the soul looks at them, they open a world, and this is the realm of touching. The sexual organs are no longer sexual organs but antennas, fingers far more delicate than ours, and which go further than our hands will ever know how to go. True touching at last, which will not stop at the form of things, at their never-broken surface, but reaches to the very fabric, to the breath and the point where life makes its entry into matter. To move so, one into the other, is to forget what moves; it is to work on the forms of the body until they get out of the way; it is to call out, to knock at the door and to call out again. And the answer will come . . .

To look at our movements! But in the making of love, don't they occur at the moment when we cannot reflect? We are like drunken people! . . . I have not spoken of reflection. It's not a question of thinking, it is a question of looking. I have asked that we look. And this is a deed of the spirit, ever so delicate. It is like an imperceptible change in distance. It consists in finding in our movements not what they meet—sensations or obstacles—but what they are made of. If we assume this distance it will become evident, simply evident, that we are not there for sheer pleasure. And then, the pleasure will grow, and we shall know that it is only a means. The means of procreation—and all couples have known it as that with a lump in the throat; but another work also, a work more secret, and that is our work today.

The noises that rise at those moments from our throats and from our chests, are hardly ever words. And in fact, of what could we speak then? But we don't sing either. We are never amazed at it. And how is it that such an acute happiness does not make us sing? On the contrary, we moan and we groan. Is this a form of lamentation? For surely these are not cries of pain. Then of what? But of work! We are at work, and how good it is to know that!

It is to displace our bodies that we move so to the densest and the deepest. It is in order that they will no longer be where they are, that we receive them, at this point, as they are. It is to allow the shell to break open. It is to allow other forces to come to relay their forces. It is for other bodies to add themselves to ours. It is so that unity might be re-established with the cosmos, but also with us. It is to recreate simplicity. Perhaps it doesn't much matter what it is! The essential thing is to work, to see ourselves at work.

It is so difficult to animate the body, so difficult not to keep the soul on one side and the body on the other, and it is such a great need to combine them that one has to try. It sometimes seems that we are doing something quite different, and that our bodies are in those moments, more than ever, struggling all alone. But it isn't true, it cannot be. Nature is extending her hand. In love she is giving us such courage. She enables us to be strong without even thinking about it. She melts over us a power of which we are devoid in other moments of our lives—yes, even those moments of emotions and dreams. In love, she plunges us to such an extent into our bodies that we shall be able to leave them.

So, let us move, let us work in pleasure. Not simply wait for it to bring its fatal result: its end. Let us be called. And if we do not know yet what is calling us, if it has no name, if it is a mystery, let us love this mystery and watch it coming towards us. You see clearly that it is impossible to be a realist in love. Love exists only to force us to be something other than what we are. It is much more than reality.

Love is great, but the soul is so small. Goodness gracious, I know well that it is small! It is not a possession we hold, it is a possibility. It is not yet today, but it could be tomorrow. And that is why I do not cease to say "one must," "one must," "we must" . . . Did I say too many "we must?" I seem to be looking for a moral. But it isn't a moral: it's a rescue.

Now, what would happen if we were the only ones, if we were only a few, to dream of the soul in love, if all the others thought of love as something tranquil, generally pleasant, and in the last resort not difficult at all; and if they didn't care to find out where it came from and where it is going; if they thought that the soul was settled ever since it hasn't been interwoven seriously with the heavens by anyone, what would happen? What would happen if, instead of looking at oneself in love, they were satisfied by looking at others and finding that to be, all things considered, insignificant? What would happen if they started making love in foursomes, or a hundred, passing partners along, one puff each? Where would we go if love were made for health reasons only, and doctors became its priests? What would we put in its place, if one day love were fully known, finished? It would be a time of laziness. There would no longer be any hope, there would not even be any anger, there would not be love standing upright . . . Well, is this time approaching? I do not know. I don't have an answer for everything.

8

How will I manage to tell you harmful things about faithfulness, I who desire it so much with you? And that is not all: I who have seen so well the brightness and tenderness of it, I who have so often experienced it as the presence of a third being in love, a being without duration and without hands, who only looks, who looks at us both and cleanses us to the very heart of our being. I love faithfulness: it prevents love from aging. Nevertheless I know that it is a folly.

It says to men and women: "you think of yourself as fragile. But you are not as fragile as you think. You won't be so any longer." And up to this point it's perfect: they have such a terrible need to hear these things. But it also says: "You will not change. You must not change." And this time I am afraid, I am afraid that they will be deceived, I am afraid that all this will simply end in a lie, in lies that we will say in order to obey fidelity, and others, that we will say in order to disobey without knowing it. And I'm not sure which ones will hurt more.

This thrust that takes hold of two people by the small of the back, the nape of the neck, and all their past, and makes of their past a present, which throws them into a perpetual present, and makes them get up every day as if it were the day of their birth, makes them believe that they are for each other, forever a surprise. This great blow that falls on them and which we call love, what must one do with it in order that it last? It is so good to receive it. What must we do for it to come and hit us again every day? Should we kneel down, enclose it in our heart and make promises to it? Is that it? Are we really made in such a way that promises will keep it? That is what we believe when we are very young (actually, that was not so long ago that we believed it). But isn't it in fact unbearable to say to oneself: "I love, but it is by accident?" Previously we had not known such a displacement of forces, such light on us, and we would say quietly: "It is only for a day!"

And then our fragility, at the beginning of life, we are not ready to admit it, but rather deny it. It is now or never. It is the first opportunity and the last. The love that we share, we will share it forever. Nothing proves this, it's not even probable; but we will live it. It cannot be said that the greatest news that has ever come to us will leave us as our dreams vanish when we return to sleep. That woman is the one I love. If her love for me diminishes, it means that my love for her has diminished. If my love diminishes, then I diminish. It's a question of happiness, of happiness forever. More is at stake than that: to save ourselves. For what doesn't last, condemns us. We shall not be able to say to what, but we are threatened. Everything that ceases suddenly damages. And everything that ceases little by little, that's even worse: it ruins. As far as love is concerned, of all departures it is the greatest and if it doesn't reach its goal . . . panic takes hold of us. We shall have to promise.

Very young—I am coming back to it—we're not made to try, but to found. At twenty, what is not definitive is a joke, in quite a few cases it is even dirty, and at best it is a sadness. And so a love which would say: "let's see," it is a piece of life that one tears apart and allows to rot in a corner. Faithfulness! That is in the youth category. And the reason for this is very simple: it is because it is a challenge.

To change one's mind, when one is very young, can only be done if one does so without knowing it. But to change one's needs, one's desire, after having loved, to love no longer, that is a massacre. That is why so many young people today really frighten me: they think they have the right to try. To try love, they can, they could, but only on condition that every time they ignore that it is an attempt. And in order to start again, they should wait for the day when their hearts and their bodies have forgotten that not so long ago, they had met the absolute. This condition is so stern that every offense, as I see it, disfigures them.

Faithfulness is a challenge, for at age twenty the body goes too fast: it unravels love while making it. Love is there completely, and it is not there. Either it is dreams, or it is consumption. But in the dreams love is untenable. If we allowed it to have its own way, it would be the love of no one. It would be the love of the night, of the woman, of the departure, of ourselves. The girls and the revolutions would only have one face. Remember: it is no longer to know whom one touches. And for the dreams there is too much body. Love is not born. I mean that it has not yet come down into our gestures. It is caught up there, in the region which is that of the soul and to which we are still so near, that we want so much not to leave it.

Also to tie up together the soul and desire, at the beginning it is difficult to the point of being painful. If that had meaning, one would need time to accomplish it. One would ask that the first love be free of consequences. One would beg that it would exist only for the body (but it is never for the body that it exists). One would wish to swallow some love before giving some. Giving still leans to the side of dreams. Between one single time, immediately, eyes closed, me first, and no consequences, and the other face of love, where we will learn slowly to love, where tomorrow will hold a greater truth than today, we are cut in two parts. So we promise.

The promise of loving more every day, of loving forever, of renouncing the desire to desire for the joy of a single desire, is not a concession at twenty: it is a need. And those who have not known it have missed a step. One day one will find them settled, but incapable of respect. It is a need because it is the only means at an age when the body only lives if it eats, of forcing a little bit of soul into love. Later on . . . but I will talk to you about that later. For the moment, once again I am twenty, I am still faithful, and I believe only in eternity. I feel that a hand rests on the noise of my desires; I can sense it. It is something other than a hand; it is peace. That must not disappear. Come closer! You too will be caught again between the body that flees and the soul that stays.

The body doesn't know anymore where it is. That girl, it is she. Oh! It was she a moment ago when I made her sit close to me. No other could have taken her place. The very idea of replacing her, I would have killed that idea. It is she again, now that I embrace her, go through her, and she comes into me, and we nourish one another. It is she. I shout it to myself, I am going to shout it to the universe. And it is she no longer: she has been eaten . . .

Can one say something so ugly, so crude? But I love her! . . . I have loved her. She allowed herself to be loved. Doesn't one have to learn love? And can one know it after just once? Time, it is a matter of time. But do I have even time enough to perceive love? Of course, soon we are going to start again. But love is odious, it is wonderful, and it has its own way of blinding. Next time, will we not be separated again?

Us, separated! At this moment, the first in our life when we would accept death, if, as a reward we could simply remain the way we are! To be separated by what unites us? It is a scandal. It is a conflagration and it has to be extinguished. Quite suddenly, the flame of our bodies has grown too much.

I need a backfire, a fire that comes from someplace else—any place—where nothing is ever destroyed. And she is still there, not another, but she. How could I have confused her with any woman? She is not simply a woman; she is my woman, my wife. How could I have thought that pleasure was love and that it came from anybody? It is her that I love. I love her still. I tell her so.

It is innocence. Or rather, because desire is never impersonal enough to be without shame, it is all the innocence that we can imagine in it. It is duration. I have chosen this unique woman, although my instincts want me to go towards all of them. It is sweetness: I imposed it on myself, although all the voices of love were violent. It is religion in love. An arbitrary religion, because I have chosen without seeing, without knowing, because I have chosen to limit my experience. But it doesn't really matter! We have gone through the ceremony. She and I, we have done it; and it is purity. I will now be able to touch my wife. She will be like my mother: touched–untouchable. And I will be her first child: stroked—untakable. Faithfulness gives back to us what in desire was too sudden, each time that we bumped into it. Desire is the cutting edge of a razor: it cuts off the past, it cuts into the future, and it finds only itself bearable. Yet we have to continue.

Faithful. We shall recognize one another from morning till night and from one desire to the next. Won't that be a deliverance? We will only have one life, one piece of fabric. We will be cut out of the same fabric. Every time that I will be with my wife again, she will be the same, she will be me. She will not distinguish me anymore than I will distinguish her—right down to her clothes which will be my clothes, right down to her voice which will sound in my throat. I will not go towards her. What for? Will she come towards me? Union, innocence, that's it, no longer to know that the other exists. Faithful, we will not be of one flesh: we will have no flesh any longer. A strange permission! We will be finished with division. Desire will no longer burst between us. Its curtain of fire will no longer fall between our mouths, between our hands. We will never have to bounce around again.

From one bounce to the next, it is life which uses itself up. There is something frightening in desire: it doesn't continue, it is reborn each time. Yet we must continue. How can we bear in the long run that the other always remains the other, becomes the other again at each approach, is the other with the same stubbornness that one never possesses—and doesn't want to renounce it. If my wife is faithful (and she has promised and I believe her), she is no longer herself, she is me. And our children will be "us." They will know where we are. And tomorrow is dawning. We just have to last.

But I too have promised. I surely did. And yet if I did not keep my word, faithfulness would not be dead. It is she, it is the woman who nourishes it. There is no justice there. No, in fact there is none. The woman is the guardian of time: it is her calling. She is always the one who stays. And if she stays, purity is saved. But also property. Wait! It is so unpleasant to say this. We would have to find other words. Faithfulness is not only a promise to remain what one is: it is also a promise to keep what one has taken. There may have been good reasons; but if they cease to be good reasons, one holds on all the same. One guards the treasure (that is called virtue). Even if God were to reclaim it, one would not give it up. It is the honor of the faithful, it is their sternness. One becomes jealous out of honor. One becomes jealous out of love. We cut the life out from around the one that we love because we have loved him, because we have loved her. Because we have loved the other, we don't ask any longer whether we love now. That is why I said: property.

To continue is fine. It is perhaps better than to bounce around. Providing one knows how. But we know how to continue only when we possess. Jealousy is miserliness, but faithfulness is jealousy. When has it not been so? This man, that woman that we keep, do we know whether it is still the same being who one day made a promise to us? He or she is no longer the same, and that is why we are jealous. But if it is no longer he or she . . . oh, then it is no longer us, and fear begins. Faithfulness is innocence and the opposite of innocence.

It remains that today, promises are not fashionable, and in fact neither is marriage. Soon there will only be provisional marriages. Should we bemoan that? But if our societies are provisional, if our civilization can no longer prove that it will still exist in thirty years, and if all our young people are certain that it will no longer exist, why would one want them to promise to last? The only way of saving marriage today, is to make it provisional. It is to tear it out of the domain to which it didn't belong: that of the absolute. For the absolute was not the domain of marriage: it was the domain of society.

In the past, to whom did couples vow to remain together forever? To their church, which made a commandment of it; to their country, which in exchange protected them; to their parents, who did their best to remain together; to the family, which was stronger than all the families; to the children, who would come and would in turn create a world, but a world similar to theirs; namely faithful. It was to the future that they were giving their promises; to the future, because they knew it already; to everything which was not themselves, because it existed in itself, self-sufficiently, was sufficient for them, made them proud. They didn't promise anything to themselves; they were hardly involved. If they got married, they didn't settle their own destiny, but rather the destiny of others. They would marry so that the world might continue. But what if it didn't continue? . . .

All right, most probably it will continue and its only condition is perhaps our own anxiety. And the millions of young people who are ready to opt out might perhaps   just be afflicted by an illness that is so feeble that one dares hardly mention it: lack of imagination. At least they are rational in no longer being faithful. And in fact, is that the case? It seems to me that they wish to be faithful in another way.

Thirty years ago, a man was condemned if he left his wife. Our parents would have condemned him. We feel sorry for him, we feel sorry for them both; at least we understand them. The younger ones, they simply take note. It doesn't surprise them. They don't ever ask if these two were married, but how they were married. And it would not take much for them to ask why. If they were to learn that it was because of the love of order, to increase fortune or security, to obey habits or conventions, or simply for no other reason than that marriage, after all, is marriage—then they would not give it a further thought. It's outside of their world. They are bothered by all these stories of duration, and this business of possession disgusts them. Are they wrong?

They are wrong not to hope any longer. But today, in order to hope, does one still have to do it as in the past? There are crumblings and ruptures that keep you alive better than the desire to last. And if everything is falling apart, doesn't one have to be the first to dissociate oneself? They dream of it.

I see that they are still dreaming—and even of faithfulness—but differently. They are always making promises to one another (how could a boy and a girl do without them? The discovery in itself, isn't it already a promise?). But they don't say any longer: "Because you love me, love me forever." They don't use an imperative any longer. They say: "I will love you as long as I am capable of it." That might be for the entire life; it could end upon waking the next morning. Indeed the entire life. Nothing proves that it could not be a complete commitment. Why should one only love on demand? It does happen that love takes hold of you. It does happen that it is strong because one knows it to be fragile. It does happen that it may do some good to you and to others. It does happen that it is reborn every day out of its own poverty. And supposing we rid it of all pride, even of rendering it greater than ourselves, even of wishing to accomplish it in conformity with laws that we have not made; wouldn't it then have a better chance? We marry provisionally. But what if we re-married every day!

The faithfulness of young people is that of an attempt. But could it have become anything else in a world where the laws of love have been exploded? And who has exploded them? It is never young people who destroy. They are perhaps about to do so; but they haven't had time yet. The laws of love and marriage have cracked just before and because of them. Surely we are not going to reproach them for that. They will forget our morality: they do forget it. It was the only means left at their disposal to forget our failures.

The laws of love no longer exist. If only that were the case! The terrible thing is that they are still trailing along, or that surreptitiously they are being replaced. In our galloping industrial societies in the early days of a post-industrial era, all human relationships are being reforged, but without speaking about it. Laws are being remade. And it is not us, but the young people who are the first to have to endure them. From the office of the psychologist to the billboard, and from the opinion polls to a session of "sensitivity training," only one thing is said—and not said—and said again: "you have all the rights, but you don't exist." How come! Only one thing? But there are really two things, and contradictory! There are two, that's true; but also that is not said. A trick is even used to suggest that it is obvious, that they are one and the same.

"You do not exist" is implied everywhere. Or at least "you hardly exist." Which makes you believe that you don't quite resemble all the others; it is a residue. It is a residue of ancient beliefs. And those beliefs have been thoroughly tested: they did not make you happy. Your personality, that is simply the sum of your appearances, to which you add, in order to preserve a small intimate corner, the sum of your whims and your specific ignorance. The Self? The Self is admirable, and we need to cultivate it, but without losing sight of the fact that it is not solid, and that it gets in the way. By the way the "Self" is never there; it is changing all the time. You will have as much "Self" as the questionnaires we will send to you . . . You exist so little. How important is it? Didn't we tell you that you had all the rights?

I am not going to demonstrate this. I do not demonstrate: I observe. And you can see it just as well as I do. Isn't it obvious that young people live under this new law, and that they feel it? They feel it so acutely that they take advantage of it, but in fact don't want it. No one has been able to convince them that they did not exist, but half the job has been done: before them (this time they are certain), the others didn't exist. They simply have to try everything.

They try love. That's where they have had to start, and that couldn't be done without a certain amount of breakage. And breakage can frighten. But after all, they are not the ones who stack the pornography in the shop windows. I wonder even if they look at it. They experiment with love every which way. They play hide and seek everywhere. But is it worse than obeying the old laws while detesting them, and pretending that one respects them? The young people will find faithfulness in love again, not because they have wanted it or because they have been ordered to, but because without faithfulness, love does not exist. It is not a law of society: it is a law of nature. However, it will not be the faithfulness of their ancestors. That faithfulness could well have been dead—and for quite a while. The new faithfulness will be hard in a different way. It will not favor our instincts.

When will it come? I speak of it in the future, knowing full well that it is not yet born. But we long for it. Can you imagine that our love lives for yet a new hope? Thousands of couples, they too touch it already today. The hands are heavy, alas, yes! And their eyes are not opened well. But who has ever been able to see the dawn with other eyes than those of the night? This brand new faithfulness is so beautiful! It is so sudden!

Fidelity forbids hate in love; it forbids jealousy. On this account, how many lovers, how many spouses it will leave behind. Jealousy, for the majority of people was—and still is—inverted love, but it is love. It is the anger of love; and he who has no anger has no faith. Jealousy was always justified. One wept over its consequences. But one also weeps over death, which is a consequence of life. There are cases of legitimate self-defense; jealousy was one of those cases. It was sad, but innocent. And the idea that it might be a crime, namely an act which kills that which it wishes to preserve, that idea did not come to anyone. There have always been people to condemn jealousy, but they were those who condemned love. The others recommended it. They recommended it before love, in virginity; during love, in what they called possession; after love, in vengeance. It was the mad companion of the follies of love, and it was cherished.

It is finished: we no longer have a right to it. Jealousy could only be tolerated if love were bad. We have learned that it wasn't; that it could be, but then we ourselves weren't good; it is that we didn't know how to receive it. Jealousy was only excusable if we loved objects. That woman is my field. I will be the first on my field, I will grow a hedge, and no one will know what I sow there. That woman is my earth. When I plow it, it will go where I want it to go, it will have my shape, no other. That man is my rain. His clouds will only break over me . . .

Oh, sorry. Of all the objects I have chosen the most beautiful. So often, between a man and a woman, it isn't even a matter of earth.

We are not objects. Not even our bodies are such. Or rather, yes: they could become so; but love is there to prevent it. Everything related to possession belongs to the realm of things, not to our realm. That has always been said, but it was not experienced. Or, one made jealousy into a crime of the body, and of it alone, but in reality it comes from the soul, fully from the soul, and cannot come from anywhere else.

Jealousy will become hideous. It isn't so yet, it will not be tomorrow; but its ugliness is beginning. Some men and women see it. I have met them here and there for the last twenty years. They put on a different face. They have begun to love love itself. They understand that nobody had told them what it really is. They perceive it in marriage—and when it happens, they are not even surprised; in marriage, but also in adultery; in unions of a week, but also in those of a lifetime; in the most intimate inventions of couples—and that in fact we'll never guess—and in their most impersonal inventions; in what one used to call faithfulness, in what one used to call infidelity. They know that love is so difficult, so awkward, and rare, that to give it a government, a government and unique laws would be to carry out a death sentence against it. They accept everything in love, except hate.

But if jealousy is hatred there should be a way to get rid of it: that would be not to love so much. Couples would have to divide things into two clearly separated parts: feelings and sexuality. Didn't I just say that love is always awkward? It is in the "swinging clubs" of California and of elsewhere. It is in the slight hygiene of exchanges. It is in the big collective parties where no one knows anymore who he is. Those concerned tell us that they feel so much better afterwards. And in fact, they return to their habitual partner, liberated. But freed from what? They say: from boredom, from shame. And if that were from love! Love is rather rare already, it is bored enough nowadays; there was no use taking away what it had.

The new faithfulness knows that if it isn't I who loves, there is nothing. I, you. But then the circuit of possession starts all over again. It will start again, and it is not ready to die. Nevertheless, we can change it.

I love you, yes; but I am not proud of it. By that I mean that I don't take credit for it. I have not conquered you, and you have not conquered me (when will the day come when we shall no longer use military language?). We surprised one another, and that is very different. We surprise one another every day. That everything, which makes my insufficiency necessary has suddenly taken on one face only, yours; that all these difficult needs (unbearable even, because if reduced to myself, I would never be able to solve them) have suddenly met equal needs, yours; that is the real surprise. And in order that we might feel it for a long time, do we really need promises? It is surprise and recognition that make love. Everything else destroys it. And when surprise disappears there won't even be duties anymore.

And so I will never tell you that I will love you forever. I really don't know. I will tell you that today I long for it to be so. This permission, this opportunity to live in love, one through the other, I hope that they will last. They will last if we never think of them as a right. In loving me, you have given me no right, unless it be surprise. I will still often call you "my love" and—why not—"my wife." But it will be the "my" of wonderment. It will mean: "how good it is that you still wish to stay!" And in fact you will stay, I know that you will, as long as we prefer the love which traverses you and me, above all that we make of it.

For you today (you tell me so and I believe you), it is through me that love passes. But if it should happen that one day it will be through another? And that has already happened: love has come to you through other men, it has come to me through other women. How about beginning by loving them, those others! Because jealousy is first of all retrospective.

It is understood: nowadays people are no longer fanatical about virginity, and purity has changed sign. But as of their loss, I wonder if we do anything but to comfort ourselves in forgetting it. Actually, we should not forget it. If I do not like everything that has happened to you, the worst and the best, the transient and what still lasts after it has ceased, everything that the others have erased from you, and all their traces, the novelty and the age of your dreams, the nudity of your body and all the clothes with which your memories cover it, if I do not like this gift of yourself which you have given to others, it is then that I do not love you. I shall certainly not love you for very long because I would love only a persona. There will be your usefulness (you see, that is horrible! your usefulness for me). There would be this small, diminished being, this little person that I have reduced to my love, to my use. There would be you reduced to my measure, who have become what I want now, what I am capable of figuring out. You would be my present. What a good deal! But what will you be tomorrow? And if you are ever only what I am becoming, what is the good of having met?

No, I prefer to love you the way the others have seen you. I know what is in my own interest, I prefer to love what you have lived, and how you have lived it. To the love which I feel, I will one day prefer (I really think that I will) the one that you feel. That will demand a tremendous effort, an effort, but after all nothing else. It won't require that I renounce myself, that I make myself very small. On the contrary, it will require that all at once, I enlarge myself. It doesn't promise me half a life, but two lives: yours and mine. I wonder if to have loved each other, was to have lived twice!

That's all right for the past. But tomorrow when others will come into your life, into my life (because after all, that might happen), that is where we have to be strict. It is so easy to say: "Nobody will ever come." It will be more than easy: it would be good. It would seem good. It would resemble love. But supposing it were the very opposite and supposing it were at last the opportunity to show how faithful we are!

You understood me correctly, in a new sense. Because usually faithful means: "Because I give you everything, you owe me everything." Usually, to give is only a word which we abuse, it is only the name of our demands. Do we ever give anything else than what we need? At best, we give what we are. But even that, we only do it unevenly little by little. We do it at the beginning; we do it when there is a danger. The rest of the time we do not give: we ask. And then each one of us is only a very small piece of the universe of men, of the universe of women. How can we possibly imagine that we can be sufficient for everything when we can't even be sufficient to ourselves? You will have needs that don't belong to me. Will you have to do away with them? Renunciation is not the medicine of desire. In the present state of humanity it is a remedy that does more harm than good. You could receive from another what I would like to give to you, but do not give you. It is even possible that another would bring you one day what I would refuse to give you. And how can we be certain that our refusals are always merits? Sometimes they are for poor reasons. And if you come back to me I will not call you unfaithful.

One says this, but nature resists. On the one hand we will know, on the other we will do. Yes, there will be accidents. But so many elements are involved in a decision. We have decided that faithfulness is not a matter of the body, knowing too well that it is larger than the body. There can't be an accident, there will be fewer and fewer of them.

Except the accident which has no return: departure. We have to be ready for that one if someone is faithful in the way I have outlined. That doesn't mean that one should think of it every day, or hope that it will happen. Heaven forbid! It does happen that two people want to be together for the whole of life (perhaps we will want that too) and that they cannot live otherwise. But everything is at stake at the moment of marriage. That day, it would be sufficient if we said that, instead of imposing on one another, we lend ourselves to each other. A loan is perhaps all that we can do, and it is surely closer to love than all the commandments. "I will be there as long as I am able and as long as you would wish it. Not an hour longer." Now that is a promise. And if one has to be made to faithfulness, a last one, for it to be faithfulness, let that be it! But if the moment comes where it has to be kept, it will be kept. There will be no forgiveness. For the less one promises, the more one has to keep the promise.

Departure was only a scandal in the old mentality: that of possession. It is true that in the new mentality it can create just as much suffering. The love that goes away necessarily creates suffering. But the old pain of departure, of jealousy, of scorn, of shame, only led to death. It was simply true that the love of the past, which one thought one had lived, one denied it. It didn't exist because now it exists no longer. What stupidity! What one didn't see was that love, successful or not, is work. Not comfort: work. Work done on us, with or without our agreement, more so than what we do ourselves.

In the old marriage (and may our expectation of the new not make us forget it), work was also involved. Today we refuse possession. But if men and women in the past wanted to possess one another, wasn't it in order to lend strength so that they might bear their condition? Was it not that without it, nothing in love would have belonged to them? The instruments of love were not theirs. Their reasons for loving one another were never quite their own: they were those of their God, of their country, of their heritage. They had only one right, to stay together, to have children together as it was commanded, to go through time, to tighten the knots of resemblance, to carry a little further the good state of things, to give to the earth a profile that will not surprise anyone. And their faithfulness was hard and beautiful. Why would they have dreamed of a change?

Love was not made for them. It wrapped them up sometimes (far be it from me to say that we have invented happiness); but that happiness was only an encouragement. What at other times, in the life of couples, was not courage became madness. It was the ruin of order. That simplicity has not gone too far away. I still feel a taste for it, and even some nostalgia. True, one didn't learn love in one generation. One didn't have leisure for it; one wouldn't have allowed it to oneself. Not all at once, not on one's own behalf. But perhaps it was learnt from century to century. To forget oneself was certainly an important piece of work. To forget oneself in order to know, to love so naturally that one didn't have to ask if one were loving, that must have been a consolation. But it is too late. Something else has begun.

Today love belongs to us. We have persuaded ourselves of that. This freedom is perhaps not as just nor as true as the abandonment of centuries gone by, but it is ours, and courage, today, is to live with it.

We still want children, but their arrival is not fatal. It also happens that we don't want any. From day to day we seem to know less and less whether to call them is a duty, or only a pleasure. A pleasure, well, yes! In most cases it is only that. Because no one is able to tell us what the earth will be like in twenty years, what human beings will look like. Maybe humanity is just on the verge of letting its power burst out. But it is equally possible that it could suffocate or fall asleep. Love has always been a wager. What shall we do if it became a threat?

The new element has suddenly appeared, this yes or this no to the species between which one has to choose. This element contains an anxiety so new that we have not had time, neither the one nor the other, to really look at it, let alone to draw its consequences. We would need to think of ourselves.

That love has so poor a goal does not seem acceptable. But when I say: "to think of ourselves," I mean: of the other. The other is the child who has to come or not come. This time there is no one to give us the answer. The event of birth is no longer totally outside of us. That is a change which makes us tremble. There is no longer truth, there is no longer error, or rather it is we who will commit them. The other, it is the man or the woman as always. Nevertheless, they are not the same. They have a new task: to love the other outside of his function, to love him for what he is, and not for the use that we can make of him. To think of oneself, to think of love, to forget its fruits and only to see the act of loving. Will humanity be able to do that? It is a task that humanity has not been taught. It is the opposite of egoism; but is humanity ready to make that distinction? It is an asceticism which, by its rigor, is worth the asceticism of the tribe, of duration, of sacrifice. But how can couples be led not to prefer themselves—what am I saying—not to prefer everything to love?

In the old marriage the sexes opposed one another. The woman looked after the house, the man looked after the street. Sometimes they opposed one another to the point of scorn. If there hadn't been the weight of traditions and the erosion of habits, they would have not tolerated each other. If there hadn't been the ritual of maternity, outside the seasons of love they would have hated one another. They were so determined to preserve their differences that they took them for decrees from heaven. Love was but a truce that nature gave them, but which was not decided by human beings. Love was a bonfire: it was a brush fire. It was too difficult to live, to be able to live together.

But in the new marriage, it will be necessary to bring the war to an end. Men and women will have to discover that there is no man and there is no woman. Each sex is defined; it is defined in its forms, its means. But that is only the manifested part. In that part which is not revealed, it is already the other sex. What a man accomplishes, a woman has always already dreamed it first. Audacity, one might believe, is the virtue of men. But it is the principle of femininity. As for the forgiveness, which is said to inhabit the heart of women, it is the man who is made to give it, because only he can forget. The society of men, and their fixity—it is women who wanted them. The imaginary capricious world of women—it is always the men who desire it.

The time has come to understand that there is a man in a woman and a woman in a man and that each being has to work for the whole of its life before knowing its name. But nothing will be resolved through imitation. Not a single step will have been made if one day all the boys are taken for girls and all the girls for boys. The distance to cross is not one of dress. It is not even one of laws and professions. Not a single claim will open the door to the mystery. If each one of us is the other secretly, then the task will have to be done in secret. And there is only love to accomplish it.

The great picture—you know well, the one that I have spoken to you about so much—it was not you: it was you in me. But I didn't invent you, I didn't construct you piece by piece: you were there. And the same is true for your great picture, because women have one too.

A child will be born to us; it must be. But that child will be "us." And we will have to bring it up as one does with all children of the earth, without knowing too much where he will go, and without ever getting weary.

Neither you nor I will be as we were before we met. It is far too sad in the end never to change. If our love keeps us as we are, then we mistook it for love, but that wasn't really it.

Our child will be us, but he will be a genuine child: the day will come where we shall no longer recognize him. And if for his own sake we must let him leave, then we will let him leave. May that never be necessary! Nevertheless, to be united, that is really what it is: to be capable of separation. Anyway, people don't ever separate. I have not left anyone. No one has ever left me. It is work, which one fine day was accomplished in a different way.